"Easy to read, understand, and apply, this work provides a practical approach to responding to the literacy problems most commonly encountered in the classroom. Farrell and Mathews lead us across the bridge from research to practice."

—**G. Emerson Dickman, Esq.**
Immediate Past President
The International Dyslexia Association

"This text is absolutely needed . . . will fill a *huge* gap in my workshops [and] truly give our teachers of struggling readers something to 'sink their teeth into' and make a difference with their students."

—**Jean Schedler, Ph.D.**
Schedler Educational Consulting

"A much-needed, comprehensive resource for teachers striving to address the underlying language weaknesses of students who struggle with reading comprehension . . . an extremely valuable tool for planning and implementing targeted interventions."

—**Eileen S. Marzola, Ed.D.**
Education Consultant
Contributing author, *Multisensory Teaching of Basic Language Skills, Second Edition*
Immediate Past President, NY Branch of The International Dyslexia Association

"Looking through the powerful lens of differentiated levels of language development in three older students with learning disabilities, Farrell and Matthews deliver research-based guidelines and effective remedial approaches for improving both the content and processes of comprehension instruction."

—**Judith R. Birsh, Ed.D.**
Editor, *Multisensory Teaching of Basic Language Skills, Second Edition*

"By focusing on three students in three educational placements, Farrell and Matthews have given us a book that truly moves from research to practice. . . . The clear, concrete, and practical examples of differentiated instruction make this book a 'must have' for every teacher in today's inclusive classrooms."

—**David C. Winters, Ph.D.**
Department Head
Department of Special Education
Eastern Michigan University

"Reminds us that although a multiplicity of neuro-environmental factors contribute to successful reading acquisition, educators armed with solid knowledge and effective approaches can make a big difference. Read the book; your students will benefit!"

—Gordon F. Sherman, Ph.D.
Executive Director
Newgrange School and Education Center
Princeton, New Jersey

"This book is a definite must-have road map to improving a student's academic achievement and functional performance."

—Paul F. Barbato, Psy.D.
Director of Special Services
Dumont Public Schools
Dervitz Education Center
Dumont, New Jersey

"Extremely valuable . . . provides insights into critical contributors to reading comprehension while identifying accompanying assessment and instructional activities that are differentiated based on individual profiles of students with reading disabilities."

—Nancy Hennessy, M.Ed.
Former President
The International Dyslexia Association
Educational Consultant
Co-author, *LETRS Module 6: Digging for
Meaning: Teaching Text Comprehension*

Ready to Read

Ready to Read

*A Multisensory Approach to Language-Based
Comprehension Instruction*

by

Mary Lupiani Farrell, Ph.D.

and

Francie M. Matthews, Ph.D.

·P A U L·H·
BROOKES
PUBLISHING C?®

Baltimore • London • Sydney

Paul H. Brookes Publishing Co.
Post Office Box 10624
Baltimore, Maryland 21285-0624
USA

www.brookespublishing.com

Copyright © 2010 by Paul H. Brookes Publishing Co., Inc.
All rights reserved.

"Paul H. Brookes Publishing Co." is a registered trademark of
Paul H. Brookes Publishing Co., Inc.

Typeset by Aptara, Inc., Falls Church, Virginia.
Manufactured in the United States of America by
Sheridan Books, Inc., Chelsea, Michigan.

All examples in this book are composites. Any similarity to actual individuals or circumstances is
coincidental, and no implications should be inferred.

Purchasers of *Ready to Read: A Multisensory Approach to Language-Based Comprehension Instruction*
are granted permission to photocopy the blank forms on page 74 and Appendix B for clinical or
education purposes. None of the forms may be reproduced to generate revenue for any program
or individual. Photocopies may only be made from an original book. *Unauthorized use beyond this
privilege is prosecutable under fedral law.* You will see the copyright protection notice at the bottom
of each photocopiable page.

Library of Congress Cataloging-in-Publication Data

Farrell, Mary Lupiani.
    Ready to read/by Mary Lupiani Farrell and Francie M. Matthews.
       p.   cm.
    Includes bibliographical references.
    ISBN-13: 978-1-59857-051-9
    ISBN-10: 1-59857-051-X
    1. Reading—Language experience approach.   I. Matthews, Francie M.   II. Title.
    LB1050.35.F37 2010
    372.43—dc22   2010015290

British Library Cataloguing in Publication data are available from the British Library.

2014   2013   2012   2011   2010

10   9   8   7   6   5   4   3   2   1

Contents

About the Authors

Mary Lupiani Farrell, Ph.D., earned her doctoral degree from Teachers College, Columbia University. She is a professor at Fairleigh Dickinson University, where she has served as Director and Associate Director of the School of Education and Director of the Learning Disabilities Program. She currently directs the Center for Dyslexia Studies, which offers the nationally accredited Dyslexia Specialist Orton-Gillingham Training Program for teachers as well as related services to struggling readers in the community. Dr. Farrell is the university director of the Regional Center for College Students, a comprehensive support program for undergraduates with learning disabilities. She is State Director of the New Jersey Masonic Children's Learning Centers and serves on the Executive Committee of the International Multisensory Structured Language Educational Council (IMSLEC). Dr. Farrell has presented on the topics of reading and training teachers to teach reading at the state and national levels and has authored articles on a range of topics. She maintains a small private practice in Ridgewood, New Jersey, specializing in teaching reading to students with dyslexia.

Francie M. Matthews, Ph.D., holds a doctoral degree from the Communication Sciences and Disorders Department at Northwestern University. She is the founder and director of a learning center specializing in the diagnosis and treatment of dyslexia and other language-based learning disabilities in Westfield, New Jersey. She has worked with children and adults with language learning differences for 25 years through her center, public schools, and clinical settings and has a long-standing interest in the relationship of oral language abilities to literacy. Dr. Matthews has presented on the identification and treatment of reading disorders at the state and national levels and has authored several articles on this topic. She is a recent past president of the New Jersey Branch of The International Dyslexia Association. Dr. Matthews also served on the Board of Trustees of the Winston School in Short Hills, New Jersey, a school for students with learning differences.

CHAPTER 1

Introduction

This is a book whose time has come. Much has been written about the basic skills of word recognition and fluency. However, basic skills are merely the means toward the goal of comprehending text for learning and enjoyment. It is important that teachers and parents understand that it is also necessary to address, and often remediate, skills students must employ beyond this basic level to successfully comprehend text. We distinguish these other skill areas from basic skills by referring to them as "higher level" and include vocabulary, morphology, syntax (sentence comprehension), and reading comprehension in this group. While instruction in these skill areas is typically ongoing with work on basic reading skills, it may be difficult to attend to these areas in the early stages of teaching since learning the code is the first priority and instructional time is limited. Therefore, one purpose of this book is to familiarize the reader with the higher level reading skills students need for schoolwork and lifelong reading and to illustrate common standard and remedial approaches to teaching these skills to students with reading disabilities.

Because the focus of this book is on students with reading disabilities, each of whom presents a unique profile of learning needs, we believe it must address methods for planning instruction to meet individual students' needs. Case histories of Cindy, Jim, and Bill, three very different students who struggled with acquiring basic reading skills, will be discussed throughout the text to demonstrate how research-based intervention approaches may be selected and adapted based on an individual student's needs for remediation in higher level reading skills.

There is a broad spectrum of oral language skill in the population of students generally referred to as reading disabled, and it is largely this component around which higher level reading instruction must be adapted.

All three students have had difficulty learning to read despite having average or above average intelligence and the availability of at least adequate to good instruction. Yet, as the reader will see in the brief individual descriptions presented below and again in the lengthier descriptions at the end of this chapter, the students vary widely in terms of their oral language ability and therefore require very different approaches to higher level reading instruction.

Jim is a student with consistently good oral language skills who fits the profile of the classic dyslexic, described by Shaywitz (2003). He had difficulty learning to decode, but his good oral language skills helped him compensate and reading comprehension comes fairly easily to him. Billy, too, originally had difficulty learning to decode. Even though his reading accuracy has improved, subtle oral language difficulties affect his reading comprehension. Cindy is a student with continuing word recognition problems and also multiple oral language problems that interfere with comprehension.

We present our three students as fifth graders after they have already had substantial decoding instruction and more instructional time becomes available for addressing higher level reading skills. The specific research-based interventions we propose for each student are based on our clinical judgment, their test results, and our experience with comparable students. Recommendations are also governed to some extent by the type of school environment in which students are served. Jim is placed in a general education classroom. Too high performing to be eligible for special education services, he does have a 504 plan as mandated through the Americans with Disabilities Act Amendments Act of 2008 (PL 110-325) through which he is eligible for standard accommodations, such as extended time for test taking. He has outside private tutoring. Billy is classified as having a learning disability and is placed in an inclusive classroom, in which, typically, a special education teacher collaborates with a general education teacher to augment instruction for a small group of students with learning problems. Cindy is also classified as having a learning disability. She is placed in a pull-out replacement reading/language arts program and has a somewhat modified curriculum in those subjects.

The scientific literature on reading and speech and language includes studies on students described with a variety of diagnostic labels, including dyslexia, language learning disability, specific learning disability, reading disability, and other terms. There is great overlap in the use of these terms. We have chosen to use the term *reading disability* throughout the text to refer to our three students because that is the problem that they share and which the book hopes to address. Catts and Kamhi (2005) justified the use of the term *reading disability,* stating that it is a common term used by researchers and practitioners to refer to a heterogenous group of children who have difficulty learning to read. Because of the disparity in the samples of students in studies on reading disabilities, clinicians must "cherry pick" the literature to find studies which treat students most like their own in order to identify effective instructional approaches. They often have to use clinical judgment to tweak methods described in the literature for the individual student for whom they are planning. As clinicians, we hope to illustrate this process in the differential selections we make for our three students.

Finally, the reader should keep in mind that we are presenting a large menu of objectives and related prescriptions for each language area for each student. It would not be feasible to fulfill every recommendation for any one child due to constraints in time and resources. Teachers will have to carefully select what they choose to apply.

Readers should expect to gain an understanding of the following:

- Framework of the higher level reading skills of vocabulary, morphology, sentence comprehension (syntax), and comprehension

- Dimensions of oral language and the relationship to higher level reading skills

- Standard classroom approaches to teaching higher level reading skills and research-based strategies for adapting them for students with reading disability

- High-frequency areas of difficulty for students with reading disabilities and research-based strategies for addressing them

- Methods for selecting and adapting remedial methods based on students' oral language ability

We complete Chapter 1 by introducing the reader to our three students. Chapter 2 provides a brief overview of oral language and a more detailed description of our students within that framework. Chapters 3 through 6 each address a different higher level reading skill—vocabulary, morphology, syntax, and reading comprehension. Each chapter includes the following information:

- Definition and related terms

- Relationship of the specific skill to reading

- Brief description of development

- Standard classroom approaches to instruction

- Frequently used strategies for adapting classroom instruction for students with reading disabilities

- Research on difficulties and interventions reported for students with reading disabilities

- Formal and informal methods of assessment

- Differential application of treatment strategies—illustrated through case histories on our three students

Now it's time to meet our students.

BILLY

Billy's birth and family history is uneventful. Except for his frequent ear infections, his parents had few concerns about their firstborn son. They lived in a small town in Indiana where they owned and operated the local grocery store that had been in the family for years. Billy's mom and dad had been high school sweethearts and had married right after high school. They both worked in the family business. Billy was an active baby and began walking before his first birthday. His mom became concerned by the time he was 2 that he wasn't saying enough words. She got to know many of the 2-year-olds who came into the grocery store with their families and recognized that they had a lot more to say than Billy did. She mentioned her concerns to the pediatrician, but he assured her that Billy would soon grow out of it. In fact, his vocabulary did improve considerably after a myringotomy, a surgical procedure for clearing fluid buildup from his ears resulting from frequent ear infections.

Billy enjoyed going to the local preschool program. He was well liked by the other children and the teachers. He sometimes had difficulty being understood because of the way he articulated words. However, he was generally successful and had learned all the letter and number names by the time he completed preschool. His kindergarten teacher noticed that Billy was having a great deal of difficulty with tasks such as rhyming and identifying the beginning sounds in words. He began receiving school-based speech and language therapy in kindergarten for his articulation and sound awareness difficulties.

By second grade, Billy's articulation had improved, but he was falling behind in reading. His teacher referred him for an evaluation by the school child study team by whom he was diagnosed as having a learning disability, with particular difficulty noted in the area of reading decoding. He was classified and given special education services to address these difficulties through an in-class support model.

While Billy had difficulty keeping up with his classmates on reading-related tasks, outside of school he had many activities in which he met with success. Although his fine motor skills and handwriting were poor, his gross motor skills were good and led to consistent success in sports. In the fall, he played soccer; in the winter, basketball; and in the spring, he was the star pitcher of his baseball team.

In third grade, he attended a free clinic, operated by the local university, to continue his reading instruction. His mother drove him 1 hour each way every week to get this help. By the beginning of fifth grade when we meet him for the first time, his decoding scores are approaching grade level. However, he continues to be a slow reader. Billy continues to have in-class support throughout middle school and high school, where he plays on several varsity teams.

JIM

Jim began skateboarding at 4, and with his pack of friends, had spent many summers and after-school hours cruising down San Francisco's neighborhood hills, conquering the local park's obstacles and spending days at skateboarding parks. When his family moved to New Jersey when Jim was in fifth grade, he easily made new skateboarding friends and, just like in the old neighborhood, skateboarding was the most important thing in Jim's life. Jim's mother, a freelance graphic artist, had always watched over Jim and his older sister for signs of delay in their development because her husband Art, a successful engineer, had difficulty learning to read, as had other members of his family. Jim's early years were uneventful. He had always loved puzzles and also made elaborate block structures. As her children grew, Jim's mother felt reassured because they both loved to have books read to them. Jim was not even in kindergarten, when he learned to call out the names of signs—Shell, stop—as they drove through town. Jim went to kindergarten knowing how to say and write all of the letters of the alphabet as well as the numbers up to 20.

Jim loved kindergarten. Early in Grade 1, however, Jim's mother noticed that Jim would struggle with homework on letter sound but had no difficulty with the math homework. Jim's teacher felt that there was no reason for concern and that Jim was clearly a very smart kid who would catch up in his own good time. However, on the final Grade 1 report card, Jim was rated as having mastered skills on almost all subjects except reading and spelling, for which he was rated as needing improvement.

In Grade 2, Jim excelled in most school subjects but had difficulty in reading. He always got his homework done, but his parents thought it was taking longer than it should for him to read the materials. He really disliked reading. However, because he had learned to recognize many words by sight, he continued to score at average levels on standardized reading tests given in class. Because of these results and the fact that he was achieving decent grades, his school did not feel that an evaluation was warranted. His parents found a private evaluator at the end of Grade 2. They were delighted to learn that Jim had an IQ of 128, but they were disappointed to learn their suspicions that he had dyslexia were confirmed. As the evaluator explained, Jim had high intelligence, excellent verbal reasoning ability, and strong oral language skills. His problem was primarily in lower level phonological language skills involved in listening to sounds within words, segmenting them, and learning sound–symbol associations. These results explained some inconsistencies in Jim's school performance. He appeared to easily comprehend information presented in class, but he seemed to get bogged down whenever he had to demonstrate what he knew through a writing assignment. In comparison to his oral answers, his written responses were very brief and poorly spelled.

In the summer before Grade 3, Jim began receiving private tutoring with an Orton-Gillingham approach to address his reading and spelling problems. Jim's reading and spelling improved significantly, but he had difficulty keeping up with reading assignments and also had trouble completing tests that had substantial reading involved. His classroom teachers were understanding, always permitting Jim extra time to complete tests, giving an extension on homework assignments that involved extended reading, and providing two grades on his written work—one for overall quality and another for spelling. When we meet him, at the beginning of Grade 5, he had a 504 plan through which he was officially able to get accommodations, such as extended time on tests.

With this 504 plan and private tutoring when needed, he successfully completed middle school and high school. With his outstanding verbal ability, he was well able to advocate for the accommodations he needed.

CINDY

Despite the difficulties that she had to overcome since her premature birth, Cindy has grown into a healthy, happy, and hard-working student. Cindy's mother, who had been a teacher before she stayed home to take care of her children, worried that Cindy could be at risk for learning problems because of her low birth weight and lengthy stay in the hospital. Her fears worsened as she waited well past Cindy's first birthday to hear her say "ma-ma" for the first time. Cindy's dad, a successful cardiologist at a teaching hospital in Florida, was thrilled when Cindy, at 18 months of age, called out "da-da" for the first time when he walked in from work.

Cindy loved to follow after her older brother and sister, and they were always willing to include her in their play. Growing up, Cindy loved to play in the sandbox, loved to be pushed on the swings until she learned to pump, and eventually mastered the many riding toys that spilled over the backyard. But, she especially loved the family pool—and would spend hours in one of her favorite floats. She would eventually become a competitive swimmer.

When Cindy was 2½ years old, her pediatrician, who had been monitoring her progress, recommended that she be evaluated at the hospital speech and language center, where she was given a diagnosis of specific language impairment. At the age of 3, she was classified by her school district child study team and began to attend the district's preschool program, which included speech therapy. Because this program provided only group instruction, Cindy's parents arranged to have private speech and language sessions for her as well. With the additional help, she began saying more words and sentences.

She was reevaluated prior to entering kindergarten and classified with the designation of Specific Learning Disability, given the discrepancy between her intellectual ability and her language skills. Cindy's individualized education program (IEP) had her placed in a general education class in the morning and a resource room program in the afternoon. Cindy continued with speech and language therapy two times per week throughout kindergarten. After kindergarten, she received a pull-out replacement resource room program in reading and language arts. This placement continued throughout fifth grade, and Cindy is fairly comfortable with her school program as we meet her for the first time.

In middle school, Cindy has difficulty with the change of teachers and classes, keeping track of assignments, and keeping up with assignments. Her parents explore other options and place her in a small, private school for students with learning disabilities. In this environment, she has the advantage of small classes, specially trained teachers, and an extensive support structure.

Billy and Cindy were evaluated by their school district's child study team, and pertinent results from this testing are listed in Appendix A. Also listed in the appendix are results of testing administered to Jim by a private evaluator.

CHAPTER 2

Language

This chapter covers the following sequence of topics:

- Definition of language and terms
- Relationship between oral language and written language
- Overview of basic reading skills
- Beyond basic reading skills: reading disability subtypes in the literature
- Other diagnostic issues

DEFINITION OF LANGUAGE AND TERMS

Bloom and Lahey defined language as "a code whereby ideas about the world are represented through a conventional system of arbitrary signals for communication" (1978, p. 4). Language can be oral or written. Brief descriptions of the components of language and related skills, including phonology, morphology, syntax, semantics, and pragmatics, are provided in Table 2.1. Each of these components of language, except pragmatics, is defined in greater depth in later parts of this book, and the relationship of each of these components to reading comprehension is explored.

RELATIONSHIP BETWEEN
ORAL LANGUAGE AND WRITTEN LANGUAGE

Oral language (listening and speaking) and written language (reading and writing) are alternative systems on the same continuum of communication. Written language ability, to a great degree, depends on one's oral language proficiency. While oral language develops first, the relationship between oral and written language is reciprocal in nature, and it changes over the course of development. Exposure to written text in school years and mastery of the conventions of written language influence a child's oral language system.

Although oral language and written language share many components, they are not identical. Oral language is used primarily in conversations between people and usually involves topics of everyday interest, common vocabulary, and relatively simple sentence structure. Facial expressions and gestures, as well as paralinguistic features such as intonation and volume, facilitate communication. With oral language, planning is minimized; the interactive format allows for immediate clarification if necessary. Written

Table 2.1. Language terms

Language component	Related skill
Phonology	The ability to discriminate, store, and reproduce sequences of sounds within words.
Morphology	The ability to recognize, understand, and use morphemes, the smallest units of meaning in our language (e.g., prefixes, suffixes).
Syntax	The ability to understand and use the rules that govern sentence structure (e.g., word order and the relationship between sentence units, such as phrases).
Semantics	The understanding of whole words (vocabulary) and sentences.
Pragmatics	The ability to understand and use the conventions that govern social interaction within specific contexts (e.g., how to change a topic, how to address a superior).

language is usually an individual activity. The style of written language is more formal, and the topics are often more complex. Vocabulary is more diverse and includes more literate words. Sentence structure is also more complex, often embedding several points in a single sentence. Written language requires more conscious manipulation of language variables such as sentence structure and vocabulary. It also requires a higher degree of planning since the writer must anticipate everything the reader needs to understand his message and make that clear from the start—there are no opportunities for clarification (Catts & Kahmi, 2005; Soifer, 2005).

With the advent of technology and the widespread use of casual forms of written communication such as texting, online chats, and social networking vehicles, the characteristics of written language and oral language are becoming less distinct.

This book demonstrates through our three students how oral language has an impact on higher level reading skills and how intervention must be shaped accordingly. We begin to follow our students at the point when they have acquired some basic reading skills, albeit not fully developed. The next section describes what basic reading skills are. Because much has been written about these skills, and the focus of this book is higher level reading skills, only a brief review of basic reading skills will be provided here.

OVERVIEW OF BASIC READING SKILLS

Phonological/Orthographical Processing

Before launching into our discussion of basic reading skills, it is necessary to present information on processes—phonological and orthographical—which underlie the ability to read words.

Phonological processing, particularly phonemic awareness, is an important oral language skill underlying word recognition. Phonemic awareness is the recognition that spoken language is comprised of individual sounds. This awareness is critical to the development of reading because it provides the framework for making sense out of the alphabetic or written language code. Phonemic awareness allows children to sound out and blend words when reading and to segment the constituent sounds of words when spelling. Phonemic awareness ability is a strong predictor of reading success in the beginning learning-to-read phase. Phonemic awareness ability, in fact, accounts for as much as 50% of the variance in reading achievement in children who have completed first grade (Adams, Foorman, Lundberg, & Beeler, 1998; Blachman, 1991).

Other phonological processes involved in word recognition include phonological memory (the ability to hold onto oral information for processing) and naming speed (the ability to efficiently retrieve the verbal label for a printed symbol). Phonological memory and naming speed foster internalization of letter–sound relationships and application of this knowledge to reading.

Orthographic awareness and orthographic memory (recognition and memory of significant written letter chunks in words, e.g., *ch unk*) are also important to the development of basic reading skills (Hook & Jones, 2002; Wolf, Miller, & Donnelly, 2000). These skills are important for rapid recognition of written words.

Word Recognition

Competency in word recognition results from using a variety of strategies—sounding out letters through knowledge of sound–symbol relationships (phonics); comparing features of a new word to those of a familiar word, such as *led/bed* (decoding by analogy); identifying word parts such as prefixes and suffixes (structural analysis); and matching the printed word to words already stored in memory (sight vocabulary). When reading connected text, as opposed to words in isolation, good readers also use syntactic and semantic context clues to aid word recognition. Children with strong phonological and orthographical processing abilities and a variety of reading strategies easily move words into their instant recognition word bank. This affords an "expressway" to decoding and meaning (Shaywitz, 2003).

Fluency

Accurate word recognition is only one facet of basic reading. For word recognition to lead to comprehension, it must be fluent. Fluency, according to Meyer and Felton (1999), is "the ability to read connected text rapidly, smoothly, effortlessly, and automatically with little conscious attention to the mechanics of reading, such as decoding" (p. 284). Fluency involves automatic word recognition as well as proper phrasing and expression at the sentence and whole text levels (Hook & Jones, 2002).

In summary, basic reading instruction encompasses teaching students strategies to decode various types of words, guiding their development of a sight vocabulary, and providing ample opportunities to build their reading fluency. For many children, phonological and orthographical awareness will also need to be taught and strengthened.

BEYOND BASIC READING SKILLS: READING DISABILITY SUBTYPES IN THE LITERATURE

Students with reading disabilities have been described in the scientific literature of learning disabilities, reading, speech and language, and linguistics. They comprise a broad group of students, most of whom, despite normal or above-average levels of intelligence, share a common problem in the lower level oral language skill of phonological processing, which results in difficulties in the basic reading skill of word recognition and consequently reading fluency as well. However, this broad group varies considerably in oral language skills needed for success in higher level reading. It includes subtypes with diagnostic labels sometimes used interchangeably, although not truly having equivalent meanings, including dyslexia, learning disability, language learning disability, language-based learning disability, oral and written language learning disability, specific language impairment, and language impairment.

We introduce three children with reading disabilities to illustrate the continuum of oral language ability that typically appears in this group. Selected formal test results for Jim, Billy, and Cindy are presented in Appendix A. As you can see, all three students share a weakness in phonological processing, including rapid naming ability, and consequent difficulty in word recognition, word attack (measured by nonsense word reading), and fluency. They all have at least relative weaknesses in working memory. For Jim, with very strong oral language skills, performance in listening comprehension is substantially better than performance in reading comprehension—a clear marker of dyslexia. Billy appears to fall on the midpoint of the oral language continuum for students with reading disability. Billy's performance in listening comprehension is better than his performance in reading comprehension, and he would be considered dyslexic by some authors despite the presence of known mild oral language difficulty. To note the fact that these difficulties, although mild, must be addressed in planning higher level reading instruction for Billy, the diagnostic label of language learning disability appears to be a good fit. At the extreme end of the oral language continuum, we have Cindy, who was diagnosed as having specific language impairment in preschool and continues to have substantial oral language problems. To mark the fact that instructional planning for higher level reading instruction will be heavily impacted by her moderate-to-severe oral language difficulty, the diagnostic label specific language impairment appears appropriate. These diagnostic subtypes are explained in fuller detail below.

Dyslexia

Dyslexia is characterized by "difficulties with accurate and/or fluent word recognition and by poor spelling and decoding abilities" (Lyon, Shaywitz, & Shaywitz, 2003, p. 2). Individuals identified as dyslexic have a core deficit in the lower level oral language skill of phonological processing. Although children with dyslexia may sometimes show early delays in language development, these delays are generally thought to remain mild in nature (Bishop & Snowling, 2004). Oral language is typically a strength for students with dyslexia. Secondary consequences of the decoding bottleneck dyslexic students experience as they learn to read may include problems in reading comprehension and reduced reading experience that then impedes growth of vocabulary and background knowledge (Lyon et al., 2003).

Assessment that incorporates a measure of listening comprehension is a good way to both diagnose dyslexia and differentiate children with dyslexia from students with other types of language-based reading disabilities. "Classic" dyslexia is characterized by a substantial discrepancy between listening comprehension and reading comprehension. Since many schools use a traditional aptitude–achievement discrepancy for classification purposes, as opposed to the listening–reading comprehension discrepancy, some of these students fail to meet eligibility criteria for special education services. Other factors, such as poor processing speed or working memory, may depress the overall aptitude score, making it difficult to meet the required aptitude–achievement discrepancy despite obvious reading problems. These students are likely to have 504 plans through which they receive accommodations (e.g., extended time on tests that involve reading). Students with more severe word recognition problems may qualify for special education services and be classified as having a specific learning disability.

Jim's profile is consistent with this subtype. He had no delay in language development. His strengths in syntax and semantics provide considerable cues to him for predicting words and correcting errors as he decodes text. Consequently, he always performs better when reading connected text than isolated words. He is capable of understanding oral discourse or most texts that are read to him at an age-appropriate level, and frequently, an even higher level.

Specific Language Impairment

Specific language impairment (SLI) is a term used more in the speech and language domain than the learning disabilities domain to describe students who exhibit delays in oral language development that are traditionally identified during the preschool years (Catts, Adlof, Hogan, & Weismer, 2005). Many of these students begin receiving special education services in district preschool programs that include speech and language services. They are often reclassified as having a specific learning disability in elementary school.

SLI is characterized by deficits in language in the presence of normal nonverbal cognitive abilities (Catts et al., 2005). Although there is some disagreement in the literature, children with SLI are thought to have phonological processing problems underlying their word recognition problems. There is also disagreement as to whether the severity of the phonological processing is equivalent to or more severe than that of children with dyslexia, whether it is the cause of oral language problems or exists separately from them, or whether an entirely different language-based deficit accounts for both word recognition and oral language problems in students (Catts et al.).

Students with SLI have substantial and persistent problems in aspects of language that go beyond phonological processing. They have been shown to have particular problems in morpho-syntactic awareness (Leonard, 1998), which is considered a clinical marker of SLI. Children with SLI often produce only simple syntactic structures and have difficulty comprehending complex sentences. These students also have difficulties with semantics and text processing. Longitudinal studies have shown that a reading disability is an impairment "waiting to happen" for many young children with oral language impairment (Silliman & Scott, 2006, p. 4).

Cindy's profile is consistent with this subtype. Her language development was delayed. She was identified as eligible for special education services in preschool and continues to receive these services as we meet her in Grade 5. Her weaknesses in syntax and semantics leave her reliant on phonics skills, without the aid of linguistic cues, for predicting words and correcting errors as she decodes text. Her performance on reading connected text is about the same as on reading isolated words. Her listening and reading comprehension skills are comparable.

Language Learning Disability

Catts et al. reported a high degree of overlap between SLI and dyslexia:

> Because the deficits that underlie SLI and dyslexia are likely to involve contin-
> uously distributed abilities, the comorbidity of the disorders should spread its
> effects to the borderline of each disorder. As a result, children with SLI alone
> may show low normal performance in phonological processing and word
> reading, and children with dyslexia alone may have low normal oral language
> abilities. (2005, p. 1392)

In our clinical experience, we meet many students who appear to fall into this overlap category. Their reading disabilities are characterized by phonological processing disorders and mild oral language deficits. The latter may not be noticeable in their understanding and expression of oral language, but may become apparent only in their comprehension (and production) of written language. Their listening comprehension, although not always perfectly intact, is better than reading comprehension. Students with these characteristics truly represent a mix of dyslexia and mild language impairment. Students with this profile have been described as having dyslexia (Moats & Dakin, 2008), oral and written language disabilities (Berninger & Wolf, 2009), and mixed deficit (Catts et al., 2006).

Some students within this subtype may be provided speech therapy during preschool years due to articulation difficulties and may continue to receive speech services through the primary grades. With specific learning disability as their classification, they qualify for special education and possibly speech and language services. These students comprise a large proportion of the students classified as having a learning disability and provided with special education services in our public schools. They sometimes qualify for replacement reading but more often are given extra help in reading through an in-class support teacher.

Billy's profile represents a reading disability consisting of a mix of dyslexia and language impairment. His language was somewhat delayed but not significantly so. Articulation problems were addressed in speech therapy in school. Word retrieval problems persist. Billy's weaknesses in syntax and semantics are not evident in his speaking or oral comprehension, but these skill areas provide him with limited help in predicting words and correcting errors as he decodes text. His performance on reading connected text is appreciably better than on reading isolated words. His listening comprehension is better than his reading comprehension.

OTHER DIAGNOSTIC ISSUES

Other Clinical Characteristics of Students with Reading Disabilities

We have described students who fall on three different points on the oral language continuum underlying higher level reading skills. By no means will all students at these points look exactly like Jim, Billy, and Cindy. Also, as will be seen in later chapters, each student may have additional weaknesses (or strengths) in cognitive processes that exacerbate or help compensate for his or her reading disability. Weaknesses that often—but not always—accompany reading disabilities may be found in the cognitive processes briefly described below.

- *Short-term verbal memory:* the ability to hold a small amount of verbal information in mind and use it within a few seconds

- *Working memory:* the ability to hold information in mind while performing a mental operation on the information

- *Processing speed:* the rate at which easy or overlearned cognitive tasks, such as matching numbers, are performed

- *Word retrieval:* the efficiency with which a known word is accessed for expressive language

- *Executive functioning:* the ability to manage or regulate a set of basic cognitive and emotional processes, including skills such as the ability to plan and organize, to keep information in working memory, to monitor performance, to shift from one activity or mental set to another, to inhibit impulses, and to moderate emotional responses

- *Attention:* the ability to selectively concentrate on one aspect of the task while inhibiting distraction

Overlap in the Use of Terms in the Literature

Our students represent three subtypes, differing in oral language ability, that are frequently referred to as having a reading disability. As previously mentioned, these subtypes are often merged in the subject samples of research studies and any one of several different terms listed earlier in this chapter may be used to refer to a subject sample broadly different in oral language ability. This point is illustrated by Bishop and Snowling, who discussed using the label *dyslexia* to describe a very broad sample.

> In more recent literature, it has become common to use even less stringent criteria when selecting the subject population for studies so that a child may be selected as dyslexic on the basis of having a nonverbal IQ within broadly normal limits and reading skills below the 25th or 30th percentile. Such diagnostic criteria will yield a heterogeneous group of children, including some who would not normally attract clinical concern, some who have nonspecific reading difficulties, some who would fulfill ICD-10 diagnostic criteria for dyslexia, and some who would have clear-cut cases of SLI. (2004, p. 6)

Poor Comprehenders

We would be remiss if we did not distinguish a specific category of poor readers who differ significantly from those discussed above. A category of students identified as poor comprehenders, or students with specific comprehension deficit, has received a substantial amount of attention in the literature (Catts, Adlof, & Weismer, 2006; Scott & Windsor, 2000; Cain & Oakhill, 2007). Despite average nonverbal intelligence, these students have poor comprehension skills. They are not readily noticed in the classroom due to the fact that they have average phonological processing ability and consequently have no weakness in word recognition. Their reading difficulties become apparent as the emphasis in reading instruction shifts from decoding to comprehending text. It is estimated that between 5% and 10% of students have these difficulties, although it may not always be clinically apparent (Catts et al., 2006).

SUMMARY

Language, the system of oral and written communication, includes the components of phonology, morphology, syntax, semantics, and pragmatics. While oral language and written language are similar, there are some important differences between the two systems. The relationship between oral and written language is a reciprocal one that changes over the course of development. Oral language ability provides a foundation for reading skills, and in turn, exposure to written language influences oral language ability. Oral language abilities are important for the development of the basic reading skills of word recognition and fluency and higher level reading skills. Three subtypes of students with reading disabilities, distinguished by their oral language characteristics, were presented: pure dyslexia, language learning disability, and specific language impairment. All three cases are characterized by phonological processing, word recognition, and fluency problems. Students with pure dyslexia have strong oral language abilities, especially strong listening comprehension, and the ability to draw upon these skills to help compensate for their reading disorder. Students with language learning disability have a mixed reading disability stemming from both dyslexia and mild language problems. Students with specific language impairment experience a range of oral language problems beginning in the early stages of language development, with problems in morpho-syntactic awareness being primary. These language problems undermine their reading development.

Subsequent chapters of this book will demonstrate how the instructional needs of students with these oral language/reading profiles can be met.

CHAPTER 3

Vocabulary

This chapter covers the following sequence of topics:

- Definition of vocabulary and related terms
- Relationship of vocabulary to reading
- Development of vocabulary
- Vocabulary instruction in the mainstream classroom and guidelines for adapting it for students with reading disabilities
- Research on vocabulary difficulties and interventions for students with reading disabilities
- Formal and informal assessment of oral vocabulary
- Differential application of treatment strategies to students: our three students

DEFINITION OF VOCABULARY AND RELATED TERMS

Vocabulary knowledge can mean many different things. In its broadest sense, it refers to all the words an individual can understand or use in spoken and written form. Further delineation of vocabulary knowledge refers to the modality involved. Receptive vocabulary refers to words the individual understands when heard (oral vocabulary) or read (reading vocabulary). Expressive vocabulary refers to words the individual uses in speaking (oral vocabulary) or writing (writing/spelling vocabulary).

Words in our vocabularies differ in the depth to which we know them. Initially, words are known at a surface level consisting of an understanding of the object, action, or situation to which the word refers. Eventually, words are understood at a deep level in which terms associated with a word become part of the word's meaning, and the word becomes part of a rich network that includes the meaning of all of these related terms. For example, the word *apple* is eventually associated with the words *fruit, skin, red, trees, sweet, crispy,* and *tasty.* Another layer of meaning refers to a word's connotation, or the feelings connected to the word. For example, *apple* may suggest apple pie and evoke feelings of holidays, home, and comfort.

Isabelle Beck provided yet another perspective on vocabulary knowledge in classifying words as Tier 1, 2, or 3 according to their frequency of occurrence and breadth of usage (Beck, McKeown, & Kucan, 2002). Tier 1 words are common words used extensively in everyday conversation (*baby* and *sad*). In contrast, Tier 3 words are used infrequently and often restricted to specific areas (*element* and *biome*). Tier 2 words are high-frequency words that can be used in many contexts. Beck recommended that school vocabulary instruction emphasize Tier 2 words (*astonish, gleeful*).

Students' vocabularies vary in terms of the types of words they know, the depth to which they know them, and their mastery of words across the modalities of listening, speaking, reading, and writing. While no student has equal ability across all four modalities, students with reading disabilities are especially likely to exhibit discrepancies among them. For most students with reading disabilities, oral vocabulary is stronger than reading or writing/spelling vocabulary. As we meet our three students in Grade 5, they have already had extensive instruction in decoding and spelling that, it is hoped, has facilitated their growth in reading and spelling/writing vocabulary. The purpose of this book is to demonstrate how to design instruction that accompanies or follows decoding/spelling instruction according to students' oral language ability. Differentiating oral vocabulary instruction, therefore, is the focus of this chapter.

RELATIONSHIP OF VOCABULARY TO READING

Oral vocabulary influences reading in several ways. It plays a role in children's ability to decode. A young child's phonemic awareness, a building block for decoding, is facilitated by his or her oral vocabulary. It is theorized that children develop phonemic awareness by making mental comparisons between similar-sounding familiar words (*pin* vs. *pit* vs. *pig*). Children who have more words in their vocabulary are better able to make these important comparisons (Metsala & Walley, 1998). A broad oral vocabulary also allows children to recognize whole words more easily when reading. As children read, they use print, context, and linguistic cues to match words in their oral vocabulary to the printed word. The larger their vocabulary, the easier it is to find the appropriate match, and hence, get the meaning from what they read. The depth of word knowledge, or connectedness between related words in children's oral vocabulary, also plays a role in decoding and fluency. For example, reading the word *coat* facilitates the later reading of *glove* since the latter word will have been activated through the internal meaning connections (McGregor, 2004).

Oral vocabulary plays an important role in reading comprehension as well (Carlisle & Rice, 2002; Hiebert & Kamil, 2005; Lehr, Osborn, & Hiebert, 2004; Roth, Speece, & Cooper, 2002). In fact, vocabulary knowledge has been found to be one of the best predictors of reading comprehension abilities at all grade levels (Anderson & Freebody, 1981; Roth, Speece, & Cooper, 2002; Thorndike, 1973). Depth of word knowledge, in addition to breadth of vocabulary, plays an important role in reading comprehension because word meanings that are part of a rich network are more quickly retrieved when reading. Beck, Perfetti, and McKeown (1982) asserted that automaticity of access to word meanings, rather than mere vocabulary size, is important to reading comprehension.

It is largely held that the relationship between vocabulary and reading comprehension becomes reciprocal in nature at some point in the reader's development (Seigneuric & Ehrlich, 2005). Vocabulary is initially developed by hearing words in spoken conversation. In later years, a greater number of new words are encountered through reading. A good vocabulary supports reading comprehension, and exposure to new words through reading, in turn, increases vocabulary.

The reciprocal relationship between oral vocabulary and reading can result in a vicious cycle: readers lacking adequate oral vocabularies struggle to achieve comprehension; because they don't understand what they read, they avoid reading; and because they don't read much, they don't have an opportunity to see and learn new words (National Early Literacy Panel, 2008). Whereas good readers become even better readers and learn more words, poor readers become even poorer readers and learn fewer words (Stanovich, 1986).

DEVELOPMENT OF VOCABULARY

Word learning begins with "fast mapping," in which a child picks up an initial impression of the word's meaning from context. Gaining a deeper knowledge of the word is a lengthy process dependent on the child hearing the word in many different contexts, as well as the child's overall level of cognitive and linguistic development.

The oral vocabulary of the average 6-year-old is approximately 8,000 words. During school-age years, children learn approximately 3,000 words a year or at least seven new words a day through exposure to new words in their home environments and especially through school-related experiences such as classroom discussion and reading texts (Cunningham, 2005).

Poor readers are typically delayed in vocabulary growth as a result of lack of exposure to words in text. For example, Carlisle and Katz (2005) indicated that in Grades 2 or 3, a poor reader might average 10 pages per day for 100 days of the school year, covering a total of 100,000 words of running text, while a more able reader might read 20 pages per day, perhaps doubling the number of words to which he or she is exposed.

Children with reading disabilities vary considerably in the rate at which they learn new words. For example, Jim, with excellent cognitive and linguistic ability, will acquire new words and develop deep meaning for them more rapidly than Billy and Cindy. Some of the factors that affect vocabulary growth and overall language learning in students with reading disabilities are listed below.

- Initial level of oral vocabulary. Students with a better fund of word knowledge benefit from listening more than those with smaller vocabularies. This, in turn, helps them build their oral vocabulary. For example, Cindy, with a poorer fund of word knowledge than Billy and Jim, will learn fewer words when exposed to the same oral language experience than the other two students.

- Phonological processing ability. Students with phonological processing problems, as well as verbal working memory deficits—both high-frequency deficits in students with reading disabilities—have more difficulty in learning words.

VOCABULARY INSTRUCTION IN THE MAINSTREAM CLASSROOM AND GUIDELINES FOR ADAPTING IT FOR STUDENTS WITH READING DISABILITIES

Vocabulary instruction, a customary part of general classroom reading instruction, may vary according to the reading program used and, to some extent, the teacher's experience and interest in word learning. When literacy texts or individual books are read in the classroom, teachers often identify key vocabulary ahead of time (either using the words recommended in the teacher's manual or their own judgment) and plan vocabulary instruction around these. Beck, McKeown, and Kucan (2008) endorsed the use of classroom reading materials as "authentic contexts" for use in vocabulary development and recommend a two-step approach to introducing these new words to vocabulary development: 1) a brief introduction prior to reading new words that might interfere with comprehension and 2) vocabulary lessons that may include a larger set of words with the objective of getting the words into the students' working vocabulary (p. 23).

Beck et al. (2008) provided additional guidelines for introducing new vocabulary:

- Provide "friendly explanations" for new vocabulary words, involving complete sentences that use the target word in familiar contexts as opposed to dictionary definitions (p. 23).

- After they have been introduced, plan to present new vocabulary words in additional contexts so that students can generalize the meaning.

- Provide many opportunities to "actively process" the word meanings with frequent review (p. 27).

In some classrooms, a cognitive strategies approach, such as semantic mapping, may be used to build deep meaning. In this approach, students relate new words to known words. By explicitly identifying the relationship between the words, they build a rich meaning network. Semantic maps are particularly helpful for developing understanding of abstract nouns. Table 3.1 presents specific steps for constructing a semantic map. Figures 3.1 and 3.2 are examples of completed maps that the teacher constructed with the class when introducing vocabulary for a novel about the resistance during the Nazi invasion.

Table 3.1. Directions for creating a semantic map

1. The teacher writes the new vocabulary word in a circle on the board.
2. The teacher asks the class to provide words that go with the new vocabulary word and leads a discussion about the relationships between the words. The teacher can suggest categories to think about or encourage free brainstorming.
3. The teacher writes words on the board around the new word. As the students provide words, she may ask them to identify the category and to group words from the same category. She connects categories to the new word and then, working with the students, labels the relationship.

Another approach to vocabulary learning within the mainstream is to explore words during literature circles (small, book-sharing groups). One member of the group usually has the job of identifying and clarifying new vocabulary words for the other members of the group.

Reinforcement activities in mainstream classrooms vary:

- Literacy texts often provide vocabulary exercises in an accompanying workbook. With a novel, the teacher may create reinforcement worksheets.

- Teachers may ask students to complete sorting activities in which new words are categorized according to particular features, for example, adjectives or synonyms.

- To help children remember the words, teachers often post newly learned vocabulary on classroom word walls for the students' easy reference. Students are encouraged to use the new words in their writing.

All of these experiences help children develop rich meanings and incorporate the new words into their usable vocabulary.

The best research-based practices for mainstream classroom vocabulary instruction have been summarized by the National Reading Panel, a government-sponsored panel that synthesized the findings from studies on vocabulary. These are presented in Table 3.2.

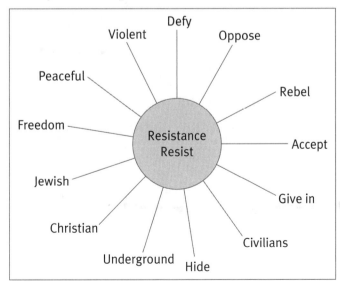

Figure 3.1. Semantic map—outcome of brainstorming.

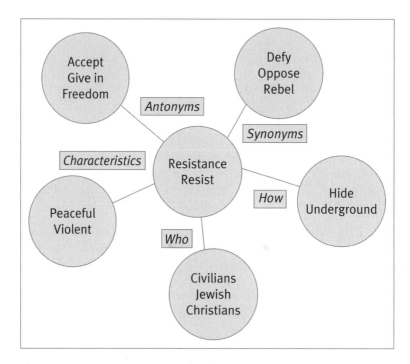

Figure 3.2. Semantic maps—identifying relationships between words.

Table 3.2. National Reading Panel's guidelines for vocabulary instruction

There is a need for direct instruction of vocabulary items required for a specific text.

Repetition and multiple exposure to vocabulary items are important. Students should be given items that will be likely to appear in many contexts.

Learning in rich contexts is valuable for vocabulary learning. Vocabulary words should be those that the learner will find useful in many contexts. When vocabulary items are derived from content learning materials, the learner will be better equipped to deal with specific reading matter in content areas.

Vocabulary tasks should be restructured as necessary. It is important to be certain that students fully understand what is asked of them in the context of reading, rather than focusing only on the words to be learned. Restructuring seems to be most effective for low-achieving or at-risk students.

Vocabulary learning is effective when it entails active engagement in learning tasks.

Computer technology can be used effectively to help teach vocabulary.

Vocabulary can be acquired through incidental learning. Much of a student's vocabulary will have to be learned in the course of doing things other than explicit vocabulary learning. Repetition, richness of context, and motivation may also add to the efficacy of incidental learning of vocabulary.

Dependence on a single vocabulary instruction method will not result in optimal learning. A variety of methods was used effectively with emphasis on multimedia aspects of learning, richness of context in which words are to be learned, and the number of exposures to words that learners receive.

Source: Reprinted from National Institute of Child Health and Human Development. (2000). *Report of the National Reading Panel. Teaching children to read: An evidence-based assessment of the scientific research literature on reading and its implications for reading instructions: Reports of the subgroups* (NIH Publication No. 00-4754). Washington DC: U.S. Government Printing Office.

Because many students with reading disabilities may have particular difficulty learning new vocabulary, classroom teachers may find the additional practices listed in Table 3.3 useful.

RESEARCH ON VOCABULARY DIFFICULTIES AND INTERVENTIONS FOR STUDENTS WITH READING DISABILITIES

Research on students with reading disability has shown that these students often have a poorer overall knowledge of vocabulary than that of peers without a disability (Jitendra, Edwards, Sacks, & Jacobsen, 2004). Because of relatively poor vocabulary, many students with reading disability frequently have less thorough knowledge of word meanings; they may recognize a word as familiar but not be able to explain its meaning correctly or to interpret its meaning in a new context. In interpreting and applying the above finding, the reader should keep in mind, as discussed in the previous chapter, that samples in the studies Jitendra et al. (2004) review included students with a broad range of diagnostic labels and an accompanying broad range of oral language ability. For example, students like Jim will have strong oral vocabularies. Billy's vocabulary knowledge will be weaker and shallower than Jim's. Cindy's vocabulary knowledge will be even more impoverished, with fewer words known at a level of deep meaning.

Research has shown a number of interventions to be successful at improving the vocabulary of students with reading disabilities, including the keyword approach, cognitive strategies, direct instruction, activity-based method, constant time delay, and computer assisted instruction (Jitendra et al., 2004). These approaches are presented in Table 3.4. It should be noted that there are many different goals addressed within the research on vocabulary improvement for students with reading disabilities. In some cases, the objective is for students to learn to decode new words; in other cases, the goal is to learn a word's definition; and in other studies, the purpose has been to teach the meaning of the words at a deep level. Teachers must select the method that best fits their students' needs.

It should be acknowledged that, in the discussion of successful interventions for vocabulary instruction for students with reading disabilities, questions have been raised about the effectiveness of three age-old approaches to independent word learning—teaching students to use the dictionary, gather meanings from context clues, and apply word analysis skills.

Dictionary

Using the dictionary poses a number of problems for students with reading disabilities. They become frustrated by the multiple definitions or unknown words used in dictionaries, and knowing the definition of a word is not always the same as knowing the meaning of a word (Fiore, Boon, & Lowrie, 2007). Also, reading and stating a word and its definition may not help in

Table 3.3. Adaptations for classroom vocabulary instruction for students with reading disability

The best choice for vocabulary instruction is to select words that will be used in a variety of situations.

If selecting vocabulary from a basal reading program, do not rely on the basal reading program teacher's manual to identify new vocabulary words to teach as new words. The publisher's list may not include important words for which your students do not know the meaning. Or, words could be included that are not useful enough to your students.

Teach 8–10 new words each week, if students can work effectively at this pace. Reduce the number of words taught each week if students are not retaining word meaning. Increase the number of words if students are easily learning the number of words presented.

Present new vocabulary through direct, systematic instruction in controlled contexts (familiar, unambiguous contexts).

Provide a good range of positive examples of using the word so that students are sure to learn the essential characteristics of the word.

Once the meaning of a new word is understood in a controlled situation, vary the contexts.

Provide vocabulary instruction several times each week. Even brief sessions can provide an opportunity for systematic practice of new words and review of previously introduced words.

Present each new word for a minimum of 10 exposures over the course of the week. Continue review until the student is able to use the word accurately in an oral sentence.

When teaching children the meaning of nouns, especially abstract nouns, help them create strong mental images of the words. Research has shown that verbs, adverbs, and adjectives, which more readily lend themselves to the creation of mental images, are learned more easily than nouns.

After introducing word meanings through direct instruction, promote further processing of word meaning by having students engage in interactive activities such as matching words with contexts, using words to complete sentences, developing mnemonics, and creating semantic maps.

Have students work in pairs or small groups for interactive activities, providing needed repetitions in a motivating, engaging manner in which students are likely to hear the word used from a variety of differing viewpoints.

Periodically revisit previously learned vocabulary to enhance long-term retention.

Keep in mind that students do not have to read books independently to build vocabulary. Students can learn words when books are read aloud to them or when they read along with an audio recording of the book. Share this information with parents; encourage parents to read to their children and to keep track of new words they discuss together.

Involve parents in vocabulary review. Explain that students need to have many exposures to new words in a variety of contexts. Provide them with a short list of words to be posted in a highly visible spot, for example, the refrigerator door, and ask them to systematically use these words during the week.

Use the vocabulary of each subject area when instructing students. For example, in history, use the term *primary document*; in mathematics, use the word *octagon*. Follow up with synonyms and eliciting questions to ensure that students understand the meaning of these words.

Many words have multiple meanings. Use direct instruction to teach the new meaning of a word before assigning the reading selection in which it is used.

Words that sound somewhat alike are frequently confused by students with dyslexia, (e.g., *consonant* and *continent*). When using these words confirm that students have the appropriate understanding.

Table 3.4.   Interventions for improving vocabulary in students with reading disability

Intervention	Description
Direct instruction	Teacher presents new words prior to reading text through explicit, systematic presentation of a word and its meaning. More effective than learning word meaning from context clues or having meaning presented when word encountered in text (Pany & Jenkins, 1978).
Keyword or mnemonic strategies	A picture is created in which a similar sounding key word and the meaning of the new word are combined. The acoustic and visual associations facilitate memory and retrieval. Compensates for difficulties in committing information to memory. Reported to be superior to traditional drill and practice methods (Jitendra, Edwards, Sacks, & Jacobsen, 2004).
Constant time delay	New words are associated with a simple definition. Multiple trials are given and feedback is provided—immediate at first and then given after a brief time delay—until mastery is achieved. If unsure, the student waits for the teacher to provide the correct answer and then repeats the response. Effective for students with learning disabilities (Jitendra et al., 2004; Hughes & Fredrick, 2006).
Cognitive strategy instruction	Students connect the meaning of new words with known words and note similarities and differences among related words. Students learn and store a semantic network of words connected by their meanings. Superior to traditional instruction (Jitendra et al., 2004) for students with learning disabilities.
Activity-based methods	Students engage in practical, concrete, hands-on learning as they interact with new vocabulary terms in discipline-specific activities. Improved content word knowledge in students with learning disabilities when compared to a teacher's presentation on textbook learning (Scruggs, Mastropieri, Bakken, & Brigham, 1993).
Computer-assisted instruction	Students learn a new word accompanied by a definition or a known-word synonym, sometimes with a pictorial and/or audio clue. Practice activities may include using the new word in drill and practice exercises and sentence completion tasks. Jitendra et al. (2004) reported mixed reviews but concluded that it enhances vocabulary for students with learning disabilities.

reading comprehension, as this activity does not permit the student to connect the new information with prior knowledge (Beck et al., 2003).

Context Clues

Bryant et al. (2003) described results for teaching struggling students to use context clues to recognize and derive meanings of new words as "equivocal"

(p. 118). Fiore et al. (2007) explained that this approach may be difficult for students with reading disabilities because it 1) is dependent on the student's knowledge of content, which may be lacking for students with vocabulary deficits; 2) requires integrating varying types of information from a passage, such as definitions, examples, and synonyms; and 3) requires many encounters with the word to learn it. Beck et al. (2002) cited several reasons from the literature regarding why this approach may be difficult for students with reading disabilities.

Word Analysis Skills

Word analysis involves learning how to break apart words and identify the meanings of word parts. Klingner, Vaughn, and Boardman (2007) cautioned that because this skill can be used only when new words contain the specific affixes that have been taught, it should be one of several strategies students have for independent word learning. They stated that prefixes are the most worthwhile to teach because they are seen in many words, there are relatively few to teach and learn, spelling is fairly consistent, and they are always found at the beginning of a word.

FORMAL AND INFORMAL ASSESSMENT OF ORAL VOCABULARY

Formal

As discussed above, students vary in their oral vocabulary. For teachers to differentiate vocabulary instruction, they must have comprehensive data from formal and/or informal assessment indicating a student's vocabulary profile (e.g., receptive vs. expressive oral language ability, oral vocabulary vs. reading vocabulary). There are a number of formal tests available for assessing vocabulary. These tests may be administered by psychologists, speech and language therapists, or educational diagnosticians, depending on the type of assessment being given. Tests differ in the manner in which they assess vocabulary. Table 3.5 lists some of the major tests used to assess oral vocabulary, the type of information that is yielded, and the manner in which the information is derived.

Informal

Teacher observation is a major informal vocabulary assessment tool. Over time, teachers become aware of students' oral vocabulary strengths and weaknesses from their classroom language use. While this is an accurate gauge for a student like Jim, it may underestimate vocabulary knowledge for a student such as Billy, who is more limited in expressive than receptive vocabulary. Furthermore, Billy's expressive language problems are exacerbated by difficulty with word retrieval, a common symptom in students with reading disabilities.

For a more systematic approach, teachers can construct informal measures, such as the one shown in Figure 3.3, in which students are asked to

Table 3.5. Formal assessment of vocabulary.

Test	Receptive (R)	Expressive (E)	Subtests/Formats
Test of Language Development–Primary–Fourth Edition (TOLD-P:4)	R	E	*Picture Vocabulary* (R)–select picture that matches orally presented word *Oral Vocabulary* (E)–provide oral definition *Relational Vocabulary* (E)–explain how two words are alike
Test of Language Development-Intermediate–Fourth Edition (TOLD: I-4)	R	E	*Picture Vocabulary* (R)–select picture that corresponds to a two-word phrase *Relational Vocabulary* (E)–explain how three words are alike *Multiple Meanings* (E)–provide as many different meanings for a word as possible
Test of Adolescent Language–Fourth Edition (TOAL-4)	—	E	*Word Opposites* (E)–provide an antonym for a spoken word *Spoken Analogies* (E)–provide word to complete an analogy *Word Similarities* (E)–write a synonym for a printed word
Clinical Evaluation of Language Fundamentals–Fourth Edition (CELF-4)	R	E	*Expressive Vocabulary* (E)–provide name for pictured concept *Word Classes* (R & E)–select words that are related from a response set of three to four words; explain the relationship
Receptive One-Word Picture Vocabulary Test (ROWPVT)	R	—	Select picture that matches orally presented word
Expressive One-Word Picture Vocabulary Test (EOWPVT)	—	E	Provide name for pictured concepts
Peabody Picture Vocabulary Test–Fourth Edition (PPVT-4)	R	—	Select picture that matches orally presented word
The WORD Test 2, Elementary & Adolescent	R	E	*Associations* (R & E)–select unrelated word from set of four words; explain why it does not belong *Synonyms* (E)–provide synonym *Semantic Absurdities* (E)–repair absurd statement by providing correct word *Antonyms* (E)–provide antonym *Definitions* (E)–provide definition *Flexible Meanings* (E)–provide two meanings for word

(continued)

Table 3.5. (*continued*)

Test	Receptive (R)	Expressive (E)	Subtests/Formats
Comprehensive Assessment of Spoken Language (CASL)	R	E	*Antonyms* (E)–provide an antonym for a spoken word *Synonym* (R)–select a synonym for a spoken word from response set of four words *Meaning From Context* (E)–infer and then explain meaning of obscure word from context *Idiomatic Language* (E)–finish idiomatic expression with one word

rate their familiarity with new words (which the teacher reads to them). This tool may be used with individual students or with groups of students. The words could be selected by the teacher based on a story or a textbook chapter that the students are about to read. Another simple informal assessment would be to have the student formulate oral sentences using new words from their texts.

DIFFERENTIAL APPLICATION OF TREATMENT STRATEGIES TO STUDENTS: OUR THREE STUDENTS

Billy

The child study team evaluation identified aspects of vocabulary as weak for Billy. Receptive vocabulary as measured by the Peabody Picture Vocabulary Test (PPVT) was found to be at the 40th percentile, which is within the average range. Expressive vocabulary (25th percentile) measured

Word	I have never heard the word before.	I have heard the word but don't know what it means.	I have heard the word before and understand what it means.

Figure 3.3. Informal assessment of vocabulary.

by a word-defining test, the Vocabulary Subtest of the Wechsler Intelligence Scale for Children–Fourth Edition (WISC-IV), was lower than receptive vocabulary. Several times during this definitions test, Billy commented that he "heard of the word, but couldn't explain it." He also reported this on the informal assessment tool. This suggests that Billy may have rather shallow understanding of word meanings. He needs to engage in extra activities to build up the deep meaning of words, specifically the connections between related words. The child study team also found that Billy had a significant verbal working-memory weakness (WISC-IV Working Memory Index = 21st percentile). This type of memory deficit in addition to his weakness in phonemic awareness makes it difficult for him to hold onto the pronunciation and meaning of new words. Billy needs many exposures to new words in a variety of contexts to develop deep meaning, and numerous opportunities to use them for the words to become part of his expressive language. Finally, Billy was observed to have word retrieval difficulties, which affect his ability to use the words once their meanings are established. Keeping all of these language characteristics in mind, the in-class support teacher selects the following areas to work on with Billy:

1. Augment classroom instruction on vocabulary.

2. Move new words into Billy's expressive vocabulary.

3. Teach vocabulary in a way that facilitates retrieval for speaking and writing.

Strategies for Augmenting Classroom Instruction on Vocabulary

- To identify words for further study, the in-class support teacher informally assesses students in her group, including Billy, on the words the classroom teacher has selected for vocabulary study from the novel the class is reading. In addition, she identifies potentially troublesome words from the classroom content area texts. For Billy, as is true for most students with reading disabilities, there are more words that he can't read than words he doesn't understand. She addresses the decoding issue by having Billy read the words daily until decoding is accurate.

- To develop understanding of the words at a deep meaning level, she provides the following instruction. These activities, of course, provide additional decoding practice as well.

    - The in-class support teacher instructs Billy to use the computer program, Inspiration, to construct his own meaning networks for each of the words whose meaning he did not know. Inspiration is a software program that prompts the making of semantic maps. It is especially helpful for students like Billy who need more assistance in developing meaning networks. The program's thesaurus option helps him compensate for his weak vocabulary and word retrieval difficulties. In addition, this tool easily allows Billy to represent meanings with concrete visual images by cutting and pasting images into the maps. This feature makes learning vocabulary a multisensory activity and therefore promotes learning. The steps for using Inspiration are similar to those described for making the semantic map on the classroom board and are shown in Table 3.6.

Table 3.6.   Steps for using Inspiration software

The steps for using Inspiration to create a web of related words to promote deep meaning for a new vocabulary word are similar to those for creating a semantic map on the classroom board:

1. Using a specific icon on the tool bar, Billy types the new word in a main circle; he clicks on the icon again to generate another circle that is linked to the main circle.

2. He types a related word in the new circle. Billy continues linking words to the main vocabulary word, as well as to the newly generated words, to build his meaning network.

3. The in-class support teacher coaches Billy to think of specific categories of words, such as antonyms or other types of word categories. She encourages him to use the thesaurus as needed.

4. The in-class support teacher then discusses the relationships between the words on the map with Billy.

- The in-class support teacher has Billy make a personalized vocabulary flash card for the words whose meaning he did not know. These cards help Billy retain the meaning connections he built through Inspiration. On the front, Billy writes the word. On the back, he writes the meaning of the word, two to three synonyms that he generated through Inspiration, and a sentence that uses the word in a personalized context. He also draws a picture or adds a picture retrieved from an electronic source to show the word's meaning. These cards serve as a resource for Billy in other language arts activities. These cards are always in blue for easy identification as the resource file.

- The in-class support teacher guides Billy in making a "means-the-same" set of cards (in yellow) to go with the deck of cards described above. She has him pick one synonym for each word and write it on a flash card. Billy plays concentration with a peer in school and also takes the deck home to play the game with his family. Cumulative review is provided through recycling the sets of words.

- For particularly troublesome words, the in-class support teacher develops a keyword-image mnemonic. For example, Billy had trouble remembering the meaning of the word *sentimental*, so the in-class support teacher creates the following keyword-image link:

  - She identifies a keyword. (A keyword is a small word that is part of the target term or a stretching of a prominent syllable—if possible, the beginning syllable, since words are stored in memory on the basis of their initial sound). The keyword for *sentimental* was *scent*.

  - She then associates the word *scent* with a story that led Billy to the meaning of sentimental: A boy smelling the *scent* of apple pie felt *loving feelings* about his grandmother because she always made the best apple pie.

  - Billy draws a picture of this association.

Strategies for Moving Words into Expressive Vocabulary

- The in-class support teacher has Billy use his "new" words both orally and in writing:

  - At an early stage, as recommended by Beck et al. (2008), she asks Billy to provide the new vocabulary word that best fits within a context which she describes. For example, to elicit the word *astonished*, the teacher asks, *How would you feel if your dog talked?* She gives Billy sentence starters and has him fill in the blank with a vocabulary word. For example, *When I got back my math test with the A+ grade, I was _____.*

  - Next, in daily review exercises, she asks Billy to use the word in sentences. She posts the words on a word wall so they are accessible.

- She sends home the word lists for Billy's parents to use in everyday family situations so he begins to appreciate the different contexts in which the words can be used.

- The teacher revisits previously learned vocabulary periodically to enhance long-term retention.

Strategies to Promote Retrieval

As stated, Billy may have trouble retrieving the words when speaking even when he seems to have learned them. When this occurs, the in-class support teacher will use some simple strategies to aid retrieval.

- The in-class support teacher had noticed that Billy can often retrieve the word when he waits, so she encourages him to pause and think.

- When Billy retrieves a word on his own, he has often said that it helps him to think about a situation in which he has heard or used the word before, so the teacher encourages him to try to visualize situations in which he has heard the word in order to remember it.

- If the above strategies do not facilitate recall, she provides him with the initial sound of the word he is searching for to prompt recall. It is theorized that words are stored in memory on the basis of their phonological features, so the initial phoneme cue can trigger a like-sounding word.

Jim

The private evaluator found that Jim's expressive oral vocabulary is advanced (WISC-IV Vocabulary Subtest = 99th percentile). He has mastered a large core of Tier 1, Tier 2, and Tier 3 vocabulary words at his grade level and beyond. He easily learns new words in oral discussions, and his strong verbal reasoning ability (WISC-IV Similarities Subtest = 99th percentile) makes it easy for him to develop concepts and establish connections between words. However, he is limited in his ability to acquire literate vocabulary words due to his residual decoding weaknesses. This is clearly seen by his relatively low reading vocabulary score (WJIII Reading Vocabulary Subtest = 60th percentile) and the difference between his oral vocabulary and reading vocabulary. Also, given his weak working memory (WISC-IV Working Memory Index = 35th percentile), it takes a great amount of practice to solidify newly learned words in his reading and writing vocabulary. Jim needs decoding support, especially related to multisyllabic words and words that have less common phoneme–grapheme components. Keeping all of these language characteristics in mind, the tutor selects the following areas to work on with Jim:

1. Improve reading vocabulary.

2. Improve writing vocabulary.

Strategies for Improving Reading Vocabulary

- The tutor develops a list of new words culled from the novels Jim is reading and his content area texts. Jim can probably learn to both decode and acquire the meaning of up to 15 words per week. Practice in reading the words is continued until the decoding is automatic.

- It is particularly helpful for Jim to study prefixes and roots. Learning to automatically recognize these word parts enables him to quickly read unfamiliar words with these parts and also derive their meaning. His strong verbal aptitude will allow him to generalize these concepts to many new words. An approach for teaching prefixes and roots will be discussed in greater length in the morphology chapter.

Strategies for Improving Writing Vocabulary

- Jim's tutor constructs a chart, essentially a vocabulary bank, of Jim's new words, for his ready reference. This helps him remember to use the words when speaking or writing and also helps him with spelling for the latter.

- Jim should be encouraged to use technological support (spell check) when writing so that his poor spelling does not inhibit his use of the new words in writing.

Cindy

Child study team testing found Cindy's receptive vocabulary to be within the average range (Receptive One-Word Picture Vocabulary Test = 37th percentile). Cindy's vocabulary on a comparable subtest of expressive language was much lower (Expressive One-Word Picture Vocabulary Test = 21st percentile). While she recognizes many words, she does not seem to have a broad speaking vocabulary. She scored at the 25th percentile on the WISC-IV Vocabulary Subtest, and the examiner commented on the fact that she often just provided a context for the word. This indicated that she does not have a solid understanding of many word meanings. In addition, Cindy's verbal reasoning ability was very weak (WISC-IV Similarities Subtest = 16th percentile), and this may compromise her ability to form concepts underlying words as well as to establish meaning networks between words. Finally, Cindy's verbal working memory was also found to be poor (WISC-IV Working Memory Index = 16th percentile), and this affects the rate by which she acquires vocabulary. In view of this language profile, her replacement reading/language arts teacher selects the following areas to work on with Cindy:

1. Increase understanding of Tier 2 vocabulary.

2. Increase use of Tier 2 vocabulary.

3. Increase decoding and understanding of Tier 2 reading vocabulary.

Strategies for Increasing Tier 2 Receptive Vocabulary

The in-class support teacher selects 8–10 Tier 2 words from the story the class is reading. Accordingly, the teacher selects words for which Cindy already has the underlying concept and which appear in many different domains. This selection permits Cindy to use more sophisticated words to express herself and to enhance her comprehension of oral discussions or audio recordings of text. She limits her selection to 10 because the vocabulary activities will generate additional words that may be unfamiliar to Cindy. Although many of the same strategies used with Billy could apply to Cindy, she will need more intensive and direct instruction.

-   Because of the number of repetitions Cindy needs to learn new words, the teacher selects the constant time delay approach to introduce the words as shown in Table 3.7. This approach will link a primary meaning to the word.

-   For words for which Cindy does not have any experience and is having trouble understanding, the teacher provides a multisensory activity to develop the meaning. For example, for the word *subtle*, Cindy might paint with subtle shades or taste food with a hint of flavor.

-   To give her practice with the words, as well as exposure to various contexts, Cindy's teacher uses the synonym method, with positive and negative examples as recommended by Carnine, Silbert, Kame'enui, Tarver, and Jungjohann (2006). An illustration of this approach is presented in Table 3.8 with some adaptations.

-   The teacher has her make the same vocabulary resource cards as described previously for Billy to use for ongoing review.

Table 3.7.   Constant time delay procedures for teaching vocabulary

0 time delay trial: Teacher goes through each pair of words (showing them in print for visual cues, though not expecting Cindy to read them). Teacher says new word and immediately gives synonym.

3- to 5-second time delay: Teacher randomly selects word pair and says unfamiliar word. If Cindy gives the synonym with fixed delay interval, teacher praises her. If Cindy fails to provide an answer or gives an incorrect answer, teacher gives the answer. Cindy repeats the answer and is praised. Each word pair is presented approximately six times within each instructional session.

One instructional session is conducted each day until mastery is achieved.

Table 3.8.   Synonym approach for teaching deep meaning

---

1. The teacher gives the new word and a familiar synonym, and then elicits a response from the student:

   Teacher: The new word is *gigantic*. It means big.

   Teacher: Say *gigantic*.

   Teacher: What does it mean?

2. The teacher presents positive and negative examples until the student makes six consecutive correct responses:

   Teacher: The new gym was the biggest gym of any school. Was it gigantic or not gigantic?

   Teacher: The house had three rooms in it. Was it gigantic or not gigantic?

   Teacher: The tree in the town square was the biggest tree in the state. Was it gigantic or not gigantic?

   Teacher: There were ants on our back porch. Were they gigantic or not gigantic?

   Teacher: The office building had 40 floors. Was it gigantic or not gigantic?

   Teacher: Timmy was the shortest child in the class. Was he gigantic or not gigantic?

3. The teacher reviews the new word and other vocabulary words taught previously:

   Teacher: Is this a vehicle? (Show a picture of a car.) How do you know?

   Teacher: Is this building gigantic? (Show a picture of a football stadium.) How do you know?

Strategies for Increasing Use of Tier 2 Expressive Vocabulary

- Cindy's teacher systematically uses these words in classroom discussions. They become part of a personal word wall that she has developed for use with Cindy. This list of words is shared with Cindy's parents for use at home.

- Cindy's teacher has her formulate oral sentences using the new words. This is always preceded by teacher modeling.

Strategies for Increasing Use of Tier 2 Reading Vocabulary

- Throughout the activities just described, Cindy has many opportunities to have the new vocabulary words read to her and to read them herself.

- To insure accuracy in decoding these words, Cindy's teacher has her read a list of the new words and monitors the number correct. Words not read correctly are practiced to mastery.

- To ensure accuracy in her understanding of the meaning of the word, the teacher presents a matching activity.

- The test of overall mastery is Cindy's ability to accurately decode the word and demonstrate understanding when reading it in connected text.

SUMMARY

In general, vocabulary refers to all the words a person can understand or use in spoken or written form. A child's vocabulary increases dramatically from toddler years to the beginning of school with the vocabulary of a 6-year-old being 8,000 words. Vocabulary continues to increase during school years at the rate of about 3,000 words per year. Vocabulary plays a role in children's ability to acquire phoneme–grapheme relationships, decode words, read fluently, and comprehend text. The relationship between vocabulary and reading is reciprocal, with oral vocabulary influencing reading skills and the exposure to new words through reading impacting vocabulary size. Poor readers' vocabulary growth is affected by their initial level of oral vocabulary, their poor phonological processing abilities which affect the acquisition of new words, and their lower exposure to written vocabulary via reading. Vocabulary is customarily a part of mainstream reading programs. Children with reading disabilities will benefit from modifications related to the words selected and the manner and rate of instruction. Research has shown a number of interventions to be successful at improving vocabulary for students with reading disabilities including the keyword, cognitive strategies, direct instruction, activity-based, and constant time delay approaches as well as computer-assisted instruction. Three age-old methods—using the dictionary, context clues, and word analysis—have not been found to be as effective for students with reading disabilities. Differentiated vocabulary instruction according to students' language profiles was presented through the case histories of our three students.

CHAPTER 4

Morphology

This chapter covers the following sequence of topics:

- Definition of morphology and related terms
- Relationship of morphology to reading
- Development of morphology
- Morphology instruction in the general education classroom and guidelines for adapting it for students with reading disabilities
- Research on morphology difficulties and interventions for students with reading disabilities
- Formal and informal tests of morphology
- Differential morphology instruction: our three students

VARIABLES IN MORPHOLOGY

Definition of Morphology and Related Terms

Morphology is the study of how morphemes, the smallest units of language that have meaning, combine to form words (Bloom & Lahey, 1978). Phonemes (e.g., /t/, /d/, /ch/) are nonmeaningful sound units; however, morphemes carry meaning. A word is a morpheme, and units that are attached to words, such as the prefix *dis-* (meaning not) and the suffix *-ing* (conveying present tense), are morphemes. Morphology gives readers the tools to decode complex words, determine the meanings of unknown words, and understand sentences. The importance of morphological awareness can be seen in the following passage from a fifth-grade literature book, in which every sentence has words with prefixes, suffixes, or both!

"Los Angeles was a flash*y* town. Lula found plent*y* of work. Most morn*ings* she left her *apartment* on East 43rd Place before sunrise, and she didn't *re*turn home *un*til the sun was long past sett*ing*" (Pinkney, 2000; italics added).

Terms to Know

Some basic terms that are important for understanding and teaching morphology are defined in Table 4.1.

Relationship of Morphology to Reading

The relationship between morphological awareness and single-word decoding (Carlisle & Nomanbhoy, 1993; Carlisle & Stone, 2003; Singson, Mahoney, & Mann, 2000), comprehension (Carlisle, 1995, 2000), and vocabulary (Henry, 1988, 1989; Nagy & Anderson, 1984) has been noted for all students. Good morphological awareness has been associated with higher levels of reading comprehension as well. As children advance in grades, awareness of

Table 4.1.   Morphology terms

Term	Definition
Base	The word or root (word part) to which a prefix or suffix is added. A base word can stand alone. A root cannot.
Affix	A morpheme attached to a base word or root (a prefix or a suffix).
Prefix	A morpheme placed before the base word or root (*dis-*, *un-*, *re-*).
Suffix	A morpheme placed after the base word or root (*-ed, -tious, -er, -ment*)
Inflectional suffix	A suffix that changes tense (*-ing*), number (*-s, -es*), signifies possession (*-'s*), or aligns subject/verb agreement.
Derivational suffix	A suffix that changes the part of speech of a word (govern*ment*).
Nonneutral suffix	A suffix that changes the way the word is pronounced (resign *vs.* resign*ation*).
Neutral suffix	A suffix that does not change the pronunciation of the word (coast vs. coast*al*).

the structure, meaning, and grammatical roles of morphemes has been found to have increased importance for comprehension, probably because upper elementary school texts have a higher frequency of affixed words. Finally, children who are able to analyze the parts in words and understand morphological relatedness among words build their vocabulary more quickly, learning two to three more words per day than children who do not use morphological analysis (Anglin, Miller, & Wakefield, 1993; Nagy & Anderson, 1984).

DEVELOPMENT OF MORPHOLOGY

With spoken language, morphological development begins at about the age of 2 and continues until school age (Brown, 1973). Earliest morphemes used by children are the present progressive morpheme *-ing*, prepositions such as *to*, and the plural morpheme *-s*. Later-developing morphemes include the comparative *-er*, superlative *-est*, and advanced prefixes and suffixes (*un-*, *dis-*, *-ment*).

Just as there is a developmental progression of morphemes in oral language, there is a pattern in the types of morphemes mastered in reading. Children usually learn to read inflectional morphemes (e.g., *-ing*) in first and second grade. The ability to read derivational suffixes, such as *-tion*, begins at about third grade, mostly because derived vocabulary words do not occur frequently in stories and books below that grade level. Generally, morphemes that make the most changes to base words in terms of pronunciation and spelling are mastered by children later (Henry, 2003).

MORPHOLOGY INSTRUCTION IN THE GENERAL EDUCATION CLASSROOM AND GUIDELINES FOR ADAPTING IT FOR STUDENTS WITH READING DISABILITIES

Instruction in the general education classroom typically consists of the study of common prefixes and suffixes in language arts workbooks. In addition, suffixes are often taught within the classroom spelling program, since there are rules to be learned when adding them to words (e.g., ride > riding; drop *e* before adding *-ing*).

Guidelines for selecting *content* for additional morphology instruction in the general education classroom are as follows:

- Select the prefixes and suffixes that give the most mileage for reading. There are nine prefixes that account for 75% of all prefixed words: *un-*, *re-*, *in-/im-/il-/ir-*, *dis-*, *en-/em-*, *non-*, *in-/im-*, *over-*, and *mis-*. There are fewer high-frequency suffixes. The suffixes *-s/-es*, *-ed*, *-ing*, *-ly*, *-er*, and *-or* account for 76% of all suffixed words (Lehr, Osborn, & Hiebert, 2004).

- Begin by teaching prefixes and suffixes that are attached to base words rather than roots, since these are the easiest for children to learn (e.g., teach*er*).

- Teach neutral suffixes that do not change the pronunciation of stems before those that do.

- If syllable types are taught, align the teaching of prefixes and suffixes with syllable instruction. For example, teach the prefixes *re-*, *pre-*, and *de-* when open syllables are introduced. Teach *mis-*, *un-*, and *dis-* when closed syllables are introduced.

- Beginning in fourth grade, introduce Latin and Greek roots.

- Initially teach Latin roots that have only one or two forms, such as *dic* and *dict*, as opposed to roots with numerous forms.

A variety of *methods* can be used for teaching morphology in the regular classroom:

- Use interactive activities (Henry, 2003).
  - Match prefixes with meanings
  - Match suffixes with their part of speech
  - Find prefixes and suffixes in single words or in words in sentences
  - Use grammatical context clues to put the correct suffix on a base word
  - Create oral and written sentences with different forms of the same word

- Capitalize on "teachable moments." Present roots related to a particular unit of the curriculum to make the study of these word parts meaningful. For example, a unit on government is a perfect time to teach roots such as *leg* (law), *jur* (law or right), and *jud* (judge).

- Provide intermittent review of morphemes. Read and discuss words that involve previously taught morphemes, using lists of words containing the morphemes and contextual reading.

- Teach the origin of roots. These explanations make the word-learning task a thinking activity as opposed to a memorizing one, thereby making the learning of roots more meaningful to students.

General Adaptations for Students with Reading Disabilities

It is helpful to recognize the trouble spots that students with reading disabilities will face when learning to read and understand morphemes in written language. Some common trouble spots are given in Table 4.2. Strategies for addressing these problems will be presented in the upcoming section on differentiated instruction for our three students.

Below are some general guidelines for adapting morphology instruction for students with reading disabilities in the mainstream classroom:

- Introduce new prefixes and suffixes at a slower pace than normal.

- Provide systematic practice through reading of *controlled* word lists and connected text of newly introduced prefixes and suffixes.

- Provide activities using manipulatives to break words into prefix, root, and suffix, so students practice segmenting words into parts.

- Provide word-building activities with prefix, suffix, and root cards so students practice blending word parts together.

Table 4.2. Trouble spots for students with reading disability

Trouble spot	Example
Singular possessive vs. plural	*girl's* vs. *girls*
Singular possessive vs. plural possessive	*girl's* vs. *girls'*
-ed (past tense) spelled differently than it sounds	*rested* /id/, *pumped* /t/, *thrilled* /d/
Vowel suffixes that change spelling of baseword	
• doubling rule	*trimmed, sledding*
• drop *e* rule	*baked, raking*
• *y-* rule	*happily*
Chameleon prefixes (different forms that mean the same thing)	*com-/con-/col-/cor-*

RESEARCH ON MORPHOLOGY DIFFICULTIES AND INTERVENTIONS FOR STUDENTS WITH READING DISABILITIES

It was generally thought that students with reading disabilities learn morphology in the same sequence as students without reading disabilities, but at a slower pace (Vogel, 1983). More recent research, however, has shown that students with reading disabilities have difficulty, as compared to students matched for reading level, with tasks such as morphological segmentation (Casalis, Cole, & Sopo, 2004) and the production of morphological forms that involve a phonological change to a word, such as *courage/courageous* (Shankweiler et al., 1995). This difficulty is attributed to their poor phonological skills and lack of reading skill (Casalis et al., 2004.) However, certain morphology skills, such as morpheme recognition, may develop independently of phonological skills and serve as a compensatory strategy for poor phonological skills (Elbro & Arnbak, 1996).

It has been suggested that teaching morphology might be especially useful with students who are not responding to phonological interventions (Reed, 2008). The limited number of studies that have addressed the question have reported that students with reading disabilities benefit from direct instruction in morphemic analysis (Reed, 2008; Vadasy, Sanders, & Peyton, 2006). Morphology interventions appear to work by directly improving word identification skills, which then indirectly enhances students' fluency, vocabulary, and reading comprehension (Reed, 2008). Learning to recognize morphemes may provide students with reading disabilities with a more efficient pathway to decoding multisyllabic words. In order to make time for morphology instruction, Reed (2008) suggested that teachers try to incorporate instruction on morphology into instruction on other reading skills as well as embedding it in content area lessons.

FORMAL AND INFORMAL TESTS OF MORPHOLOGY

Many children who struggle with decoding have adequate morphological skills with regard to oral language; therefore, their basic oral morphology will not need to be assessed. Children like Cindy who have had a history of speech and language deficiencies are likely to have weaknesses in oral morphology and may have been evaluated in this area.

Most standardized measures of morphology are found in tests used to assess oral language. While speech and language clinicians are very familiar with these tests, few teachers are. Some common assessments of morphology are provided in Table 4.3.

A common task used in these formal tests is a grammatical completion task in which one morpheme is used in a key word in an example sentence; then a second sentence is given that calls for a change in that morpheme. For example: Joe likes to *drive* every day. Today he is _____ (driv*ing*). This task is administered orally and requires a verbal response. Sometimes pictures are used to provide visual support to the orally presented example sentence.

Table 4.3.   Formal morphology tests

Test/subtests	Example of items
Test of Language Development–P:4, Morphological Completion Subtest	Complete the sentence with an appropriately affixed word: *Carla has a dress. Denise has a dress. They have two* (dresses).
Test of Language Development–I:4, Morphological Comprehension Subtest	Distinguish between grammatically correct and incorrect sentences: Incorrect: *She's the faster runner of them all.*
Test of Adolescent and Adult Language–4, Word Derivations Subtest	Complete a sentence using a form of the target word: Target word = laugh. *The play was very funny. The people broke out* (laughing).
Clinical Evaluation of Language Fundamentals–4, Word Structure Subtest	Complete the sentence with an appropriately affixed word: *Here is a mouse. Here are two* (mice).
Test for Auditory Comprehension of Language-Third Edition, Grammatical Morphemes Subtest	Select the picture that corresponds to the sentence: *The girls are walking.*
Comprehensive Assessment of Spoken Language, Grammatical Morphemes Subtest Grammaticality Judgment Subtest	Complete a grammatical analogy: *"See" is to "seeing" as "play" is to* ("playing"). Distinguish between grammatically correct and incorrect sentences: Incorrect: *Here are three* dog.

This type of morphology task requires a good degree of metalinguistic awareness, which is the ability to think about the structure of language as opposed to its content. The metalinguistic load makes tasks like this challenging for many children. It is important that testers consider whether children have the metalinguistic maturity to handle these tasks when they are tested; otherwise, metalinguistic skill level will be assessed rather than the intended morphological abilities. In the example presented in the previous paragraph, our student Billy might reply *going to the store* rather than the intended response, *driving*, because he does not realize how he is supposed to respond. Yet Billy may be able to use the *-ing* form of verbs correctly in his oral language.

To assess morphological competence in a way that requires slightly less metalinguistic analysis, sentence formulation tasks can be used. The child is given a word and asked to make a sentence with the word. Various suffixes are included in the target words. Some standardized measures, such as the Clinical Evaluation of Language Fundamentals-4, use this format. Alternatively, teachers can informally assess children by constructing their own sentence formulation tasks, requiring children to use base words with different suffixes in oral sentences. Cindy might be asked, for example, to make sentences with the words *hunt* and *hunted, children* and *children's.*

Because children with reading disorders have more trouble with written morphology than oral morphology, it is also helpful to assess their ability to read, spell, and explain the meaning and/or function of common prefixes and suffixes. Teachers should begin with the high-frequency prefixes and suffixes noted earlier in this chapter.

DIFFERENTIAL MORPHOLOGY INSTRUCTION: OUR THREE STUDENTS

Billy

Although Billy has underdeveloped expressive vocabulary, his expressive connected language, as reflected in everyday classroom interactions, appears age-appropriate. He has not had a recent speech and language evaluation. Before setting goals for morphology instruction, the in-class support teacher assessed his understanding of and ability to read the basic set of prefixes and suffixes listed earlier in this chapter.

The teacher then selected the following areas to work on with Billy:

1. Develop the ability to read, spell, and explain the meaning of high frequency prefixes and suffixes that he has not yet mastered.

2. Develop the ability to read affixed words in context.

To accomplish these objectives, instruction on morphemes for Billy is incorporated in an Orton-Gillingham lesson presented in small-group instruction by his in-class support teacher. In this framework, morphemes are introduced on the basis of the student's developmental decoding ability. Figure 4.1 illustrates an Orton-Gillingham lesson in which the prefix *un-* is

Review of prior related information

- Teacher provides a "hook" to related prior learning by beginning with a review of the term *prefix* and discusses other prefixes (perhaps *dis-*) that Billy has learned.

Introducing new material

- Teacher presents the new sound, phonogram, or rule in isolation.
    - Teacher presents a card (visual) with the prefix *un-*, saying (auditory), "This is a prefix. It says /un/. Trace it and say it. This prefix means 'not.' For example in the word (shows word) *unkind*, the *un-* means 'not kind.'"
    - Teacher asks eliciting question: "What does *un-* mean? How about the word unhappy—does it mean someone is happy or not? What part of the word tells us it means not happy?"
    - Billy looks at card (visual), and then says and blends the sounds /u/ /n/ (auditory, kinesthetic), while tracing the letters on any surface (tactile, kinesthetic).
    - Teacher asks another eliciting question to reinforce learning: "Tell me again, what does *un-* mean?"
- Teacher presents the new sound, phonogram, or rule in the context of words to read and spell, continuing to incorporate the visual, auditory, tactile, kinesthetic reinforcement just illustrated:
    - Billy reads a list of words aloud (visual, auditory) tracking his place in the list (tactile) with his finger or a card, and tracing letters, saying sounds aloud (visual, auditory, tactile, kinesthetic).
    - Teacher asks eliciting question after selected words to reinforce learning: "What does that word mean? What is the prefix in that word?"
    - Teacher dictates word.
    - Billy "echoes" word.
    - Billy "fingerspells" the word (i.e., allocates one sound to a finger). This provides a concrete, tactile mechanism through which students can segment the speech stream.
    - As Billy writes, he says the sound.
    - Teacher asks eliciting question after selected words to reinforce learning: "What does that mean? What is the name for the first part of that word (i.e., *un-*)?"

Review material already introduced

- Teacher presents cards for other already learned prefixes and phonograms.
- Teacher asks eliciting questions about some but not all of the prefixes presented.
- Teacher dictates already learned prefixes and phonograms.
- Billy says sounds while he writes letters.
- Billy reads lists of words incorporating already learned prefixes and phonograms.
- Billy spells words incorporating already learned prefixes and phonograms.

Figure 4.1.   Billy learning prefix *un-*.

> **Correct errors**
> - If Billy makes a mistake in reading a word, he is asked to trace and say the sounds.
> - If Billy is unable to retrieve the sounds as he tries to read, he is asked to trace the letters to get the sounds.
> - If Billy makes an error in spelling
>   - a visual model is provided, and Billy is asked to trace and say the letters on which he erred.
>   - two more examples using that pattern are immediately dictated.
>   - Billy is asked to say the sounds as he writes.

introduced. The Orton-Gillingham principles of instruction as reflected in the lesson are summarized below.

- Multisensory strategies that provide simultaneous visual, auditory, tactile, and kinesthetic reinforcement are used to introduce material (e.g., sounds, prefixes, spelling rules, syllabication patterns), review material already taught, facilitate retrieval of already taught material, and correct errors.

- Direct instruction is used.

- Instruction is sequential and information is taught in order of difficulty.

- Instruction is cumulative and content is tightly controlled so that a student is not exposed to components not already introduced. Also, once material is introduced it is reviewed consistently.

- Eliciting questions are used to reinforce new learning, review already-presented material, and help students correct errors. Figure 4.1 illustrates how eliciting questions, when added to an introductory lesson on a prefix such as *un-*, reinforce the meaning of the prefix.

Billy experiences one of the common trouble spots in learning morphology: spelling the past tense *–ed*. Additional strategies are used to augment instruction, as shown in Figure 4.2, beginning with phonemic awareness activities that help Billy discriminate between the base word and suffix, eliciting questions that reinforce this understanding, and substantial follow-up practice to bolster memory.

Jim

Because of his strong oral language abilities, Jim already uses many derived and inflected words in his verbal communication. He has a solid, innate sense of where affixed words fit into sentences, which makes it easy for him to incorporate affixed words into his oral language. While Jim may need some instruction on the meaning and function of unfamiliar morphemes, he will likely be able to use words that have these parts without much assistance. Most of the work on morphology with Jim will be on fluent decoding and spelling of words with these affixes. Since Jim does not have in-class support, he receives this extra instruction through private tutoring.

> **Adding *-ed* that sounds like /d/ or /t/ to a word with "simple" spelling**
>
> Teacher: I am going to say a word and you tell me the suffix: *pumping*.
>
> Teacher: Tell me the base word.
>
> Teacher: Now tell me the suffix in *pumped*.
>
> Teacher: Tell me the base word in *pumped*.
>
> Teacher: Say *pumped*. Spell the base word. Add the suffix.
>
> Teacher: Spell *bumped*.
>
> If Billy makes an error (e.g., writes *bumpt*), the teacher guides him to the correct answer by asking the following eliciting questions: What is the suffix in *bumped*? What is the base word in *bumped*? Spell *bumped*.
>
> The teacher would review this level by including words of this type in dictation of single words and sentences.

Figure 4.2. Teaching the suffix *-ed*.

The tutor selects the following areas to work on with Jim:

1. Automatize his reading of words with more advanced prefixes (e.g., *chrono-*) and suffixes (e.g., *-tious*).

2. Learn Latin and Greek roots.

3. Correct trouble spots in decoding and spelling.

Given Jim's high level of intelligence, he will respond well to a conceptual approach emphasizing discovery learning to address these objectives. This approach is illustrated below with respect to roots:

- Present a list of words that use the same root (e.g., con*struct*, de*struct*ive, in*struct*, *struct*ure). Ask Jim to deduce the meaning of the morpheme from the examples.

- Have Jim read and spell words made from the root.

- Pique interest and, in turn, retention of word meanings by discussing the word histories of words that are made from the root.

- Enhance attention to these word parts by asking Jim to find words that use these roots in various kinds of texts.

- Teach morphology related to content area subjects as much as possible (i.e., *import, export* during a social studies lesson on trading).

One trouble spot for Jim will be chameleon prefixes, in which the last letter of the prefix changes based on the beginning letter of the root (e.g., *com-/con-/cor-/col-*). Chameleon prefixes expand the number of significant word parts students have to learn and make reading and spelling more difficult. A strategy for teaching chameleon prefixes is presented in Table 4.4.

Cindy

As mentioned, Cindy's morphological awareness is likely delayed relative to peers. She has simple morphemes in her oral language, such as the

Table 4.4.   Teaching chameleon prefixes

Historically, some prefixes changed form because they were difficult to pronounce when added to certain roots. For example, to make articulation easier, *sub-* was pronounced as *sup-* in the word *supposed.* The spelling of these prefixes was then aligned with the pronunciation. There are four main groups of chameleon prefixes: *sub-, in-, ad-, con-* (Henry, 2004).

The following steps can be used to teach these chameleon prefixes:

1. Teach one grouping at a time.
2. Present the most common prefix in that grouping first, such as *sub-*.
3. Read and spell words with that prefix.
4. Discuss the idea that the prefix comes in other forms.
5. Read and spell words with the other forms, one form at a time.
6. Spelling in this case is being used primarily to reinforce students' ability to read these words and the meaning of the prefix.

---

plural *-s* and the verb tense markers *-ed* and *-ing,* but not more complex suffixes. She scored at the 12th and 8th percentiles respectively on the Grammaticality Judgment and Grammatical Morphemes Subtests of the Comprehensive Assessment of Spoken Language given by the school speech and language therapist. This indicates poor awareness of morphological units in oral sentences. Informal assessment of the initial set of high-frequency prefixes and suffixes showed that Cindy did not know the basic four prefixes for reading or spelling and had trouble spelling the suffixes *-es* and *-ed.* Like Billy, Cindy will benefit from systematic instruction in prefixes and suffixes, including their pronunciation, meaning, and spelling, as part of her Orton-Gillingham instruction on decoding. Work on morphology can be expected to improve Cindy's oral language skills as well as her reading and writing skills.

The teacher selects the following areas to work on with Cindy:

1. Develop the ability to read, spell, and explain the meaning of the eight most common prefixes and suffixes.

2. Read words that have these prefixes and suffixes in connected text.

3. Develop the ability to incorporate words with these prefixes and suffixes in oral sentences.

The primary instructional procedure for Cindy combines an adaptation of the Carnine approach to emphasize the meaning of prefixes and suffixes (as shown in Figure 4.3) and the Orton-Gillingham approach, as described for Billy, to teach reading and spelling of these parts.

Additional strategies to reinforce this learning are as follows:

- Provide concrete, personalized experiences to convey the meaning (e.g., *dis-*: have Cindy *disagree, disappear, disconnect* something).

- Instruct Cindy to make personalized morpheme cards and draw pictures of example words, or use electronically generated images to help her remember the meaning of the morpheme.

Teacher	Cindy
Shows card with prefix *un-*. Says:	
This card says *un-*.	
Trace it and say it three times.	*Un, un, un.* (while tracing on table)
Un- usually means "not."	
What does *un-* usually mean?	Not.
So *unsure* means "not sure."	
What does *unsure* mean?	Not sure.
What does *un-* usually mean?	Not.
What does the word *untrue* mean?	Not true.
What does *un-* usually mean	Not.
What does the word *unclear* mean?	Not clear.
The teacher asks Cindy to read and spell words with the prefix *un-* using base words that included only letter combinations that Cindy had already learned.	

Figure 4.3.   Introducing the prefix *un-* to Cindy.

- Conduct oral exercises at a recognition level of memory, a lower level of memory than retrieval, to solidify the meaning of the morpheme (e.g., *When I get on a horse, I mount it. When I get off a horse, do I <u>dis</u>mount?*).

- Provide daily manipulative experiences with written words, such as segmenting words into morphemes, building words from individual morphemes, and matching morphemes to their meanings.

SUMMARY

Morphemes are the smallest units of language that have meaning, such as words, prefixes, suffixes, and roots. Morphological awareness contributes to both decoding and comprehension. Students with reading disability are thought to learn morphological rules in the same sequence as students without reading disability, but at a slower pace. Instruction in morphological awareness may provide an alternative means of word recognition for students with reading disability as a means of by passing phonological processing problems. Students with language learning disability and specific language impairment should be taught prefixes, suffixes, and roots through a sequential program such as Orton-Gillingham, which explicitly and sequentially teaches the meaning of these word parts and how to decode them. Instruction should begin with high-frequency prefixes and suffixes. Students with pure dyslexia and strong oral language abilities will have little difficulty in mastering the meaning of these units. Additionally, they will use many of these morphemes already in their oral expression. The focus of their instruction is on decoding of these units in text. After a brief review of the most common morphemes, their instruction can progress to more advanced morphemes, including roots.

CHAPTER 5

Syntax and Sentence Comprehension

This chapter covers the following sequence of topics:

- Definition of syntax and related terms

- Relationship of syntax to reading

- Development of syntax

- Syntax and sentence comprehension instruction in the general education classroom and guidelines for adapting it for students with reading disabilities

- Research on syntax difficulties and interventions for students with reading disabilities

- Formal and informal assessment of oral and written syntax

- Differentiating syntax instruction: our three students

DEFINITION OF SYNTAX

Syntax is the way in which words are arranged to show relationships of meaning within a sentence (Carlisle & Rice, 2002). It is one of many language variables that contribute to comprehension at the sentence level when listening or reading. In addition to understanding individual sentences, listeners and readers must recognize the meaning relationships between sentences. For example, when a subject of a sentence is a pronoun (e.g., *he*), the reader must realize that the person referred to by the pronoun was mentioned in a previous sentence. These intersentence relationships are often considered part of syntax.

Terms

Sentences can be classified into a few basic types, shown in Table 5.1, based on complexity of their overall syntax structure. The variety of syntactic components within each sentence type contributes to the ease or difficulty of sentence comprehension. There are also various types of cohesive ties, presented in Table 5.2, that provide links within and between sentences (Halliday & Hasan, 1976; Wallach & Miller, 1988). In our clinical experience, these cohesive ties, especially the reference variety, may present comprehension difficulties for students with reading disabilities.

The purpose of this chapter is not to present a course on grammar. Rather, it is to sensitize the reader to the role that understanding of syntax plays in sentence comprehension and to the particular trouble spots that students with reading disabilities have with sentence comprehension.

Relationship of Syntax to Reading

Readers construct the meaning of a passage one sentence at a time. Not only is syntactical knowledge critical for comprehension, it also facilitates decoding and reading fluency. Children are typically better able to read difficult words in context than in isolation. The clues provided by syntax help children predict which word comes next in the sentence, and thus enables them

Table 5.1.   Sentence types

Sentence type	Definition
Simple	A sentence with one independent clause (i.e., a single subject and verb) and possibly one or more additional modifiers such as an adjective, adverb, direct object, or phrases.
Compound	A sentence with two independent clauses connected by a conjunction such as *and*, *but*, or *so*.
Complex	A sentence with one independent clause and at least one dependent clause connected by a subordinating conjunction such as *because* or *although*.

Table 5.2. Cohesive ties

Type	Definition
Reference	A relationship achieved by using a pronoun for a previously mentioned referent.
	Mary is a teacher. *She* teaches second grade.
Lexical	A relationship achieved by using a synonym, superordinate word, or general term to the associated word.
	Synonym: The *boy* is climbing the tree. The *child* could fall.
	Superordinate: Take some *apples*. The *fruit* is delicious.
	General word: I gave *Tom* the keys. The *fool* lost them.
Conjunction	A relationship achieved by using various types of connectors.
	Additive: I fell, and everything fell on top of me.
	Adversative: All the numbers looked perfect, yet the conclusion seemed incorrect.
	Causal: I did not know. Otherwise, I would have stayed away.
	Temporal: She opened the door. *Then* she put her coat away.
Ellipsis	A relationship achieved by the deletion of a phrase, word, or clause.
	Verbal: Who's eating? I am (*eating*).
	Nominal: What kind of ice cream do you want? Chocolate (*ice cream*).
	Clausal: Has she done her exercises? She has (*done her exercises*).

to decode more automatically (Nation & Snowling, 1998; Soifer, 2005). It has also been shown that children who have stronger syntactical skills are better able to correct their decoding mistakes (Bowey, 1986). They use synctical awareness to bootstrap weak word recognition abilities; words that do not fit syntactically are reevaluated and corrected.

In addition to helping construct the overall meaning of a passage, strong syntactical skills can help children determine word meanings. Tyler and Nagy (1990) found that older children actively use syntactical information to monitor their interpretation of vocabulary: They check that meanings they give to words agree with the syntactical requirements of the sentence.

Early syntactical delay has been found to predict reading disabilities (Scarborough, 1990). However, the impact of syntax problems on reading may not be apparent until the syntactical complexity of the text increases beyond the reader's oral syntax skills (Soifer, 2005). For example, children with reading disabilities have been found to have trouble interpreting later developing types of sentences, such as complex sentences, which are introduced in later grades (Rice, 2003).

Working memory ability has been found to be a factor in sentence comprehension (Carlisle & Rice, 2002). As sentence length increases—with multiple phrases and clauses—the reader's working memory may be taxed. Students with poor working memory may have trouble holding onto sentence parts for processing. The breakdown in working memory then leads to comprehension breakdowns.

DEVELOPMENT OF SYNTAX

Children begin to put words together to form rudimentary sentences shortly after their first words appear, usually around the age of 2. While children talk in short units initially, they understand more than they can say (Golinkoff, Hirsh-Pasek, Cauley & Gordon, 1987). Children's earliest attempts at multi-word utterances are often two words that communicate certain meaning relationships such as location and possession (*Daddy there. Mommy chair.*). Gradually, these initial word strings become longer as children begin to express two types of meaning relationships with three-word utterances (*Mommy bye-bye car*). They also add basic inflectional morphemes such as the verb suffix *-ing* and plural *-s*. These early word strings form the basis of simple, noun–verb sentences. After the emergence of inflectional morphemes, children begin to develop different types of sentences, for example, the negative and question formats. The earliest complex sentences emerge at age 3 and are mastered by age 5 or 6. Complex sentence development continues well into school-age years, with mastery of sophisticated conjunctions (e.g., *although* and *nonetheless*) and passive forms in adolescence. Sentence length continues to increase slowly but steadily through the adolescent years at approximately one word per year. Changes in the sophistication of noun and verb phrases and the development of more advanced clauses contribute to increasingly complex syntax. In later years, exposure to more complex sentences in advanced texts and the growth of written language skills actually promote the development of more sophisticated oral syntax (Soifer, 2005).

SYNTAX AND SENTENCE COMPREHENSION INSTRUCTION IN THE GENERAL EDUCATION CLASSROOM AND GUIDELINES FOR ADAPTING IT FOR STUDENTS WITH READING DISABILITIES

In the general education classroom, most instruction in syntax/sentence comprehension occurs through grammar instruction. Such instruction is one component of balanced literacy programs and often occurs in the form of individual lessons with various follow-up activities, including assignments in language arts workbooks or teacher-made practice exercises. Many teachers use a process-writing approach to teach writing and address grammar in the revising and editing phases of writing as well. Teachers may take time to address sentence comprehension during guided reading with children or when reading aloud to the class (Cohen & Cowen, 2008). Scott (1995) recommended using both direct (controlled exercises) and indirect (guided examination of actual text) approaches to improve syntactical awareness in typically developing children.

Carlisle and Rice (2002) advocated the use of a reciprocal teaching approach in which the teacher first models questioning and clarifying strategies related to sentence interpretation and then gradually transfers the initiation of these strategies to the student. To exemplify, teachers identify potentially confusing sentences in assigned literature ahead of time; they then model self-questioning, which can clarify the sentence meaning (e.g., Who is doing the action? What happened first?). When students respond to the questions, either correctly or incorrectly, teachers may ask them to prove their answers by citing portions of the text.

Some types of sentences are more difficult to process than other types, with simple, compound, and complex sentences representing the order of increasing complexity, and therefore, difficulty. The following factors also increase sentence difficulty and should be kept in mind when selecting sentences for reading instruction (Thompson & Shapiro, 2007):

- Number of clauses within a sentence

- Number of embeddings (e.g., a simple adjective or adjective clause)

- Order in which the subject and predicate (verb) occur (i.e., active vs. passive voice)

- Number of words between the subject and the verb

Several studies have shown that training in sentence combining improves reading comprehension (Neville & Searls, 1985; Wilkinson & Patty, 1993). Sentence combining requires students to combine two or more simple sentences into one longer sentence by employing different grammatical conventions (e.g., *The cat ran. The cat is fat > The fat cat ran*). Lessons in sentence combining are frequently incorporated into general education literacy programs.

Some basic adaptations to the types of instruction cited above for children with reading disabilities in the general education setting include the following:

- Read text aloud or have students use audio books to circumvent weak decoding abilities. In addition to merely compensating for poor decoding, these practices expose children to language that is syntactically more complex than the language at their independent reading level.

- Control the difficulty level of sentences that students read. Begin with simple sentences and, in particular, with simple sentences containing only one embedded chunk, for example, a prepositional phrase. When mastery of this initial type is achieved, address simple sentences with more than one chunk. After simple sentences are mastered, proceed to teaching complex sentences.

- When teaching sentence combining, begin with a cued approach. For example, to work on cause–effect relationships provide a specific connective or "tie," such as *because*, to be used in the combined sentence. Continue with cued sentences until mastery is achieved before using an uncued approach. Present words from the sentences on separate cards so the parts can be physically manipulated. This will compensate for working memory weaknesses and also allow for easier exploration of sentence structure.

RESEARCH ON SYNTAX DIFFICULTIES AND INTERVENTIONS FOR STUDENTS WITH READING DISABILITIES

As discussed in Chapter 2, some children with reading disabilities have more oral language problems than others, with particular difficulty in morphosyntactic structures (Berninger & Wolf, 2009). While it is documented that many students with reading disabilities have poor oral syntactical abilities, there have been few studies on the types of sentence comprehension difficulties that they experience when reading. However, it seems reasonable to assume that syntactic forms that are difficult to process in oral language will cause even greater difficulty for these students when reading.

Carlisle and Rice (2002) suggested that students with reading disabilities may have trouble processing the syntactical elements listed below. Some of these trouble spots are particular to written language; others occur in oral language processing as well.

- Function words: Words like *of* and *for* are often omitted or substituted, and this can change sentence meaning.

- Cohesive ties: Connecting words such as *otherwise* and other types of cohesive ties, which indicate that the second sentence is related to the first in a specific way (see Table 5.2)

- Passive sentences: Sentences that do not follow the typical subject–verb order (e.g., *The dog was walked by the girl.*)

- Double negation: Two negative words or word parts (e.g., *She would never not be on time*).

- Auxiliary verbs: Helping verbs used along with the main verb (e.g., *We **have** been studying all night*).

There has been some research on the usefulness of certain methods for treating sentence comprehension problems of poor readers. By and large, methods that required active manipulation of sentences had the greatest impact on reading comprehension, with sentence combining being particularly beneficial (Carlisle & Rice, 2002). Manipulation activities involved in these studies included constructing sentences from scrambled words, combining short sentences into longer ones, and expanding simple sentences into compound and complex sentences. A recurrent finding in these studies was that syntactical training was more helpful to children whose initial reading achievement was higher before the training started.

FORMAL AND INFORMAL ASSESSMENT OF ORAL AND WRITTEN SYNTAX

As with morphology, most formal measures of syntax are found in tests used by speech and language clinicians. Students like Cindy, with a history of speech and language difficulties, have likely been given tests of oral syntax. Students like Billy may or may not have had these tests; and it is highly unlikely that Jim has, given his consistently strong oral language skills.

Some formal tests of oral syntax assess receptive understanding of sentences. Receptive tests usually require the student to select a picture that corresponds to an orally presented sentence. Sentences vary in terms of syntactic elements that are assessed (e.g., verb tense, types of phrases and clauses). Formal tests of expressive syntax abilities (oral or written) evaluate students' natural syntactic abilities and/or their syntactical flexibility. Expressive tests usually involve formulating sentences with a specific word, unscrambling sentences, or using syntactical devices to combine short sentences into one long sentence. The expressive tests aim to evaluate the students' natural syntactical abilities and/or their syntactical flexibility. Scott (2009) raised the question of whether it can be assumed that children who evidence expressive syntax problems in formal testing necessarily have trouble comprehending the same type of structures. This has not been conclusively demonstrated in research.

Several formal syntax tests are listed in Table 5.3. Cain and Oakhill (2007) reported that a child's metalinguistic awareness of syntax (i.e., conscious awareness of correct/incorrect syntax or ability to deliberately manipulate syntactical elements) is more strongly related to reading comprehension than his or her natural syntax ability. Thus, assessments that tap this explicit awareness level are important to use. For example, tests that use sentence combining tasks require more metalinguistic awareness than tests that use sentence repetition tasks and are, therefore, better predictors of reading comprehension ability.

There are a few formal tests that directly assess comprehension of sentences when reading. These tests use a cloze format: one or more words are missing from a sentence and the student uses both syntactical and meaning clues to complete the sentences. The quality of the student's answer can show whether he or she attended to the syntactical cues or not. Children who do not provide a word that fits syntactically in the sentence probably do not have good syntactical awareness.

Because many children with reading disabilities will not have had formal assessment of syntactical abilities, teachers will need to rely on informal diagnostic tools. One informal measure that might be used is to ask children to paraphrase typically troublesome sentence types after reading or listening to them. Teachers can also have children read a sentence with a word missing and then ask them to either provide a word that fits or select the term that will fit from a response set.

DIFFERENTIATING SYNTAX INSTRUCTION: OUR THREE STUDENTS

Billy

Because Billy's expressive language is syntactically correct, little attention has been paid to his syntactic awareness in reading. However, his teacher has observed that he has trouble understanding complex sentences when reading. She also recognizes that he often fails to identify the person to whom a pronoun refers, especially when the pronoun is not in close proximity to its referent. Finally, she realizes it is important to teach Billy compensatory strategies for his poor working memory (WISC-IV Working Memory Index = 21st percentile), which has particular impact on sentence comprehension.

Table 5.3.   Formal syntax tests, subtests, tasks, and examples

Test	Subtest	Tasks
Comprehensive Assessment of Spoken Language	Syntax Construction	Generate sentences using specified morphological and syntactical rules.
	Sentence Comprehension	Judge whether two syntactically different sentences convey the same meaning.
Test of Adolescent and Adult Language–4	Sentence Combining	Combine several orally presented words into a single sentence.
Test of Language Development–I:4	Sentence Combining	Combine several orally presented words into a single sentence.
	Word Ordering	Order orally presented scrambled words into a sentence.
Test of Language Development–P:4	Syntactical Understanding	Select a picture that corresponds to an oral sentence.
		Assesses comprehension of noun–verb agreement, tense, prepositional phrases, reflexive pronouns, embedded clauses.
	Sentence Imitation	Repeat sentences of various types.
Test of Written Language–4	None	Combine several written sentences into one written sentence.
Oral and Written Language Scales	Listening Comprehension	Select a picture that corresponds to an orally presented sentence.
		Assesses comprehension of noun and verb aspects (number, tense, person, case), embedded sentences, coordination, subordination, direct/indirect object.
	Oral Expression	Sentence completion and sentence combining requiring use of above syntactical elements.
	Written Scale	Generating written sentences according to prompts, combining sentences, elaborating sentences—all analyzed according to syntactical features that are included.
Clinical Evaluation of Language Fundamentals–4	Formulated Sentences	Make an oral sentence using a target word.
	Sentence Assembly	Unscramble written words and phrases to make a sentence; then make a second sentence with the words in a different order.

Test	Subtest	Tasks
Test for Auditory Comprehension of Language–Third Edition	Elaborated Phrases and Sentences	Select a picture that corresponds to an oral sentence. Assesses comprehension of interrogative sentences, negative sentences, active and passive voice, direct and indirect object, compound and complex sentences.
Test of Reading Comprehension: Fourth Edition	Sentence Completion	Read a sentence that has two missing words, then from a list select the pair of words that best completes it.
Woodcock-Johnson III	Passage Comprehension	Read a sentence that has a missing word, then provide a word that will best complete it.

The in-class support teacher selects the following areas to work on with Billy:

1. Develop strategies that compensate for working memory weaknesses.

2. Improve comprehension of complex sentences.

3. Improve understanding of pronoun reference.

Strategies for Compensating for Working Memory Weaknesses

- The in-class support teacher plans to incorporate strategies to compensate for Billy's working memory weakness in their work together on sentence comprehension. Teaching Billy to write key words from troublesome sentences can help him concentrate on the essential meaning. The length of text to be remembered is shorter and thereby less taxing for his working memory. Also, the act of selecting the key words and writing them is a strategy that permits deeper processing of the text and enhances his understanding. To identify the important words, the teacher models reading a sentence aloud, phrase by phrase, with expression and writes the words below the sentence.

- Typical compensatory strategies are adapted for Billy as needed and adaptations generally serve to reduce sentence length in a concrete way. For example, Billy will be taught to cross out all but the two or three most important words in a sentence when struggling with comprehension of a sentence that is too long and complex for him to keep in his working memory.

Strategies for Improving Comprehension of Complex Sentences

- The in-class support teacher selects the sentence combining technique as the method for improving Billy's comprehension of complex sentences.

She begins with exercises that require Billy to combine two sentences using a specific subordinating conjunction, such as *because, when, since,* and *if.* She uses a cued format at first in which she specifies which conjunction to use:

If   The game will be cancelled.

        It is raining.

Using a multisensory approach, the teacher initially models combining sentences orally (with the written sentences also available to compensate for his working memory weakness). Billy follows by combining the sentences orally. She next asks Billy to write the combined sentence, primarily for purposes of multisensory reinforcement. Finally, she has Billy read new complex sentences with the subordinating conjunction *if* and verifies his understanding by asking him to explain the sentence to her.

- The teacher previews classroom reading selections to identify sentences of this type so that she can affirm that Billy is transferring his understanding of this sentence structure to his reading.

Strategies for Improving Comprehension of Pronoun Reference

- To work on this skill directly, the teacher uses cloze exercises in which Billy completes a sentence by providing a pronoun in place of a missing word.

- The distance between the noun and the pronoun is minimal at first so that working memory is not taxed, and then is gradually increased.

- The teacher lays a transparency on top of classroom reading materials and asks Billy to draw a line between pronouns and their referent. This, too, compensates for his working memory weakness.

Jim

As is true of many other students who struggle to learn to decode text, Jim has become an accurate reader, but he lacks the fluency of other students his age. Because he reads sentences more slowly, he actually has to keep them in his working memory for a longer time than other students. This will not be a problem for sentence comprehension in narrative texts read in Grade 5 (or prehaps even middle school), but it may begin to be a problem with high school literature. Some expository texts will present difficulties for Jim, even in Grade 5, because they include new concepts and related vocabulary. These features combined with the more complex sentence forms will further affect his fluency, creating a load on working memory and compromising sentence comprehension.

Jim's private tutor selects the following areas to work on with Jim:

1. Improve fluency as a means to improve sentence comprehension.

2. Develop ability to monitor and repair breakdowns in sentence comprehension.

3. Develop strategies that compensate for working memory weaknesses.

Strategies to Improve Fluency as Means to Improve Sentence Comprehension

The following strategy is used to improve Jim's fluency for sentence reading.

- The tutor models good fluency practices—using proper intonation and chunking the sentence into phrases through "scooping." These exercises help Jim learn to segment sentences into meaning "chunks," thereby reducing the sentence to a smaller number of parts to store in working memory for processing.

- Jim does repeated readings of sentences from his classroom materials. This practice gradually conditions him to the difficulty level of the text and ultimately leads to improved rates of reading new material.

Strategies to Monitor Repair Breakdowns in Sentence Comprehension

- Jim's tutor helps Jim understand that he has excellent comprehension ability but that he sometimes has difficulty holding the information he is reading "in his head" when sentences become too long.

- Recognizing that a sentence is lengthy becomes a cue for Jim to slow down and, if necessary, reread.

- The tutor also instructs Jim to stop at the end of each paragraph and check his comprehension of particularly long sentences. Gradually, he will automatically incorporate self-monitoring of lengthy sentences as he reads.

Strategies for Compensating for Working Memory Overload

- Jim's tutor teaches him the key word strategy as described above for Billy. Jim is more capable of comprehending complex sentences than Billy but may occasionally encounter sentences, particularly in content area reading, that need processing in this way.

- The tutor encourages Jim to routinely underline or highlight when he reads, but gives him a rule of thumb to underline no more than two or three words in a sentence—directing him to identify the who or what of the sentence and eliminate extraneous phrases. For example, the sentence *After a moment, hearing the wind outside and feeling the cold, I decided to stay home* is reduced to *I decided to stay home.*

Cindy

Cindy's replacement reading program and her speech and language sessions are coordinated through regular meetings of the therapist and teacher. While it was possible to just focus on trouble spots with Billy and Jim, in Cindy's case it is necessary to use a comprehensive and structured approach to teaching sentence comprehension. Instruction begins with simple sentences and, at least initially, oral exercises precede the reading of sentences. Instruction continues through compound and complex sentences. Cohesive ties, which are difficult for many students, are particularly difficult for Cindy given her concrete thinking and will also be explicitly taught. Because of the overall difficulty that Cindy has in learning language, a multisensory approach will be used throughout instruction.

Her teacher selects the following areas to work on with Cindy:

1. Improve understanding of simple sentences and complex sentence types.

2. Improve understanding of cohesive ties.

Strategies for Improving Understanding of Simple and Complex Sentences

- Cindy's teacher uses one of the many multisensory grammar programs, which are highly structured and sequential and use symbols and color coding to help students master the parts of speech and their roles in sentences.

- Instruction on each of these forms begins with Cindy demonstrating understanding of the form when spoken, proceeds to Cindy appropriately using the form in her expressive language, and concludes with Cindy reading sentences of this form with comprehension. To make these exercises truly multisensory, writing sentences with this form completes the study of each form. Each stage of the sequence is reinforced by the speech and language therapist.

- In addition to implementing the grammar program, the replacement reading teacher previews classroom material for follow-up instruction. As Cindy reads these sentences, the teacher asks questions to probe her understanding of the meaning. Cindy reads: Because he overslept, the boy skipped breakfast. Teacher asks: Why did the boy skip breakfast?

- As a general rule, the therapist and teacher practice the grammar concepts with content from Cindy's life. The personal information scaffolds her understanding of the syntax.

Strategies for Understanding Cohesive Ties

- Cindy's teacher works on pronoun reference in very much the same way that Billy's teacher works on the concept with him. In cases where Cindy has difficulty, the teacher scaffolds her comprehension by formulating a comparable familiar situation and then presenting again the sentence on which Cindy had difficulty.

- Cindy's teacher also works on lexical cohesion, in which a synonym or a category name is used to refer to a previously used term. For example, "Don't eat too much *candy. Sweets* are not good for your teeth."

  - To help Cindy recognize lexical categories, the teacher creates a matching game with specific nouns in one color and synonyms or category terms in another color, for example, *vegetables* and *string beans*.

  - After Cindy demonstrates mastery in matching the pairs, her teacher asks her to read the sentences and probes for understanding.

  - The teacher links this learning to classroom reading material. As with Billy, the teacher puts an overlay on top of reading material so that Cindy can draw a line between lexical ties.

SUMMARY

Syntax is the way in which words are arranged to show meaning relation-ships within a sentence and between sentences. Sentence comprehension is achieved in large part through understanding of syntax. Syntactical awareness also supports word recognition and reading fluency. Development of syntax begins around the age of 2 when children start to use two-word utterances to express themselves. The development of complex syntactical structures con-tinues into adolescence. Certain types of sentences are more challenging for children to understand, and students with reading disabilities can be expected to have difficulties with these. Children with substantial language problems have more difficulty with syntax than other children with reading disabilities and require explicit and highly structured instruction to improve their com-prehension of written sentences. Children with mild oral language problems have difficulty with known trouble spots in syntax. Children with consistently strong oral language ability are likely not to have difficulty with sentence com-prehension when text is controlled for decoding difficulty.

CHAPTER 6

Listening and Reading Comprehension

This chapter covers the following sequence of topics:

- Definitions of listening comprehension and reading comprehension

- Relationship between listening and reading comprehension

- Development of listening and reading comprehension

- Comprehension strategies taught in general education classrooms and general guidelines for adapting them for students with reading disabilities

- Research on comprehension difficulties and interventions reported for students with reading disabilities

- Formal and informal assessment of listening and reading comprehension and a process for combining results to identify individual students' comprehension needs

- Differential application of treatment strategies to students: our three students

DEFINITIONS OF LISTENING COMPREHENSION AND READING COMPREHENSION

Listening comprehension is the ability to understand spoken language. Listening comprehension is tapped in a host of everyday and academic activities such as participating in conversations, following directions, listening to stories, watching movies, and comprehending teacher lessons. Reading comprehension is the ability to understand what is read.

RELATIONSHIP BETWEEN LISTENING AND READING COMPREHENSION

Listening comprehension forms the base for reading comprehension, yet because of the differences between oral and written language noted in Chapter 2, the processes and subskills involved in the two types of comprehension are not identical. Students begin with better listening comprehension than reading comprehension ability. As students have more exposure to print, the differences in their abilities between the two skills decrease. For narrative text, in children with no reading disability, this occurs by about Grade 2. However, listening comprehension ability remains better than reading comprehension ability for expository text until about Grade 4, largely due to the fact that students do not have the ready access in oral language to the text structures used in expository text. For students with no reading disability, reading comprehension levels are higher than listening comprehension levels by Grade 8, for both narrative and expository text.

DEVELOPMENT OF LISTENING AND READING COMPREHENSION

The development of listening comprehension is dependent on the maturation of linguistic, cognitive, and metacognitive factors. Listening comprehension requires the development of discrete oral language skills. Good listeners have strong ability in the oral language areas covered up to now in this book—vocabulary, morphology, and syntax. In addition to these language skills, a variety of cognitive processes are tapped in listening, such as auditory memory, sequencing skills, inferential thinking and the ability to recognize the organization of input. Metacognitive skills play a role in listening comprehension as well. Children must be able to identify the specific purpose for which they are listening, such as following directions, understanding a story, or comprehending the main ideas of a lesson. Over time, and as children are exposed to more listening situations, these skill areas develop interdependently and influence overall listening comprehension. Listening ability constitutes the base for reading comprehension. Weaknesses in these areas have an impact on listening comprehension, and, therefore, reading comprehension.

The development of listening comprehension is dependent on linguistic, cognitive, and metacognitive maturation. Listening comprehension is dependent on the development of discrete oral language skills. Good listeners must be able to process the sounds of words and the morphosyntactic structures of sentences and have an adequate vocabulary. Furthermore, a variety of cognitive processes are tapped in listening such as sequencing abilities, the ability to recognize the organization of the input, auditory memory, and inferential thinking. In addition, children must be able to identify the specific purpose for which they are listening, such as following directions, understanding a story, and comprehending essential aspects of school lessons. Over time, and as children are exposed to more listening situations, these dimensions develop interdependently and constitute a basis for reading comprehension.

Catts and Kamhi (2005) cited Chall's stage theory to explain the development of reading comprehension. Chall (1983) stated that in the early phases of reading development, children are "learning to read." They first acquire letter–sound correspondences and then apply this knowledge to written words. Much attention is given to the act of decoding the words—children are "glued to the print." In the next stage of reading development, children develop reading fluency and this enables them to become "unglued from the print," and reallocate their cognitive energy to understanding text. In the subsequent stage of reading development, children begin to "read to learn"; they read texts to gain information. Children usually achieve this stage around the fourth grade. As children's experience with reading increases, they become exposed to different genres of text with various text structures. This experience leads to improved comprehension of text, especially expository texts. Reading comprehension develops further during adolescence and beyond with readers being able to understand different viewpoints and analyze and form opinions from what they read.

COMPREHENSION STRATEGIES TAUGHT IN GENERAL EDUCATION CLASSROOMS AND GENERAL GUIDELINES FOR ADAPTING THEM FOR STUDENTS WITH READING DISABILITIES

As is true for the reading skill areas covered in previous chapters, differentiating reading comprehension instruction involves making decisions on the content, or "what," of instruction as well as the process, or "how," of instruction. Most students with reading disabilities are instructed in general education classes wherein the content for comprehension instruction is determined by the district curriculum. The process of instruction is governed by the needs of the whole class, with some individual adaptations (generally driven by IEPs or 504s) for students with reading disability. Therefore, it is important that both special education teachers and general education teachers be familiar with comprehension strategies frequently taught in general education classrooms and have guidelines for adapting this instruction for students with reading disability. In this section we describe the following strategies frequently taught in general education classes:

- Two comprehension strategies that guide the reader through processing of the entire text: the Directed Reading-Thinking Activity (DRTA) and the What I Know, What I Want to Know, What I Have Learned (KWL)

- A general approach for teaching a specific comprehension skill, such as main idea

- A strategy for answering test questions, that is, Question–Answer Relationships Strategy (QAR)

We follow this with information on general adaptations for teaching these strategies to students with reading disabilities. These general adaptations are illustrated through a discussion of our three students—Billy, Jim, and Cindy.

Comprehensive Comprehension Strategies

The current literature on teaching reading provides a variety of strategies for instructing children to comprehend what they read. In general, teachers teach students to use the same approaches to comprehending text that proficient readers are reported to use spontaneously. This involves actively constructing meaning through the use of before, during, and after reading strategies. Two popular approaches that address these stages are the DRTA (Stauffer, 1969) and the KWL strategies (Ogle, 1986). These approaches are typically taught in general education classrooms using an instructional process in which teachers model the approach by thinking aloud and then scaffold student applications. This is sometimes followed by students practicing in small groups.

The DRTA directs students to access background knowledge, make predictions, stop to evaluate the accuracy of their predictions, and then either adjust their thinking or generate new predictions accordingly. The specific steps that students are taught to follow are presented in Table 6.1. These steps are frequently provided to students on cue cards.

Table 6.1.   Directed Reading-Thinking Activity (DRTA)

Introduction:

Before reading, ask yourself what you already know about the subject.

Predict:

1. Look at the title and any pictures and ask yourself what you think the story will be about.
2. After reading a section, ask yourself if your prediction was correct. Prove it by finding the important places in the text.
3. If your prediction was not correct, ask yourself how it should be changed?
4. Read another section of text and repeat the process until the entire story is read.

Reflect:

After the entire selection is read, ask yourself what you found in the text to prove your predictions. Think about what caused you to modify your predictions.

Table 6.2.   What I Know, What I Want to Know, What I Have Learned (KWL)

1. Look at the title, headings, and bold words to get a general idea of what the selection is about.
2. Record what you already know about the topic in the first column of the KWL chart.
3. In the second column of the chart, write down what you want to find out from your reading.
4. After reading, write down what you learned in the third column of the chart.

The KWL strategy is especially helpful when reading expository texts. It guides students through the process of accessing their background knowledge about a topic, generating questions they hope or anticipate will be answered by the text, and summarizing what they have learned after reading. This strategy is carried out with a three-column KWL chart with the headings: What I **K**now, What I **W**ant To Know, What I **L**earned. Directions for implementing the strategy are presented in Table 6.2.

Specific Comprehension Strategy—Main Idea

Teachers often instruct children in the use of specific strategies for various aspects of the reading process. Considerable classroom time is spent teaching students how to identify the main idea, as well as how to retell and summarize what they have read. For the most part, instructional practices for retelling and summarization stem from procedures taught for identifying the main idea.

Most procedures for teaching main idea include the following steps (Carnine, Silbert, & Kameenuei, 1990; Jitendra, Cole, Hoppes, & Wilson, 1998; Vaughn & Klingner, 1999):

1. Students read text in sections (this may vary from one to two paragraphs, using controlled materials or classroom texts).

2. Students identify the subject about which most of the sentences are written (approaches may vary in terms of controlling for type of main idea, provision of prompts for students to use if they have difficulty, use of self-monitoring cue cards, etc.).

3. Students generate a sentence in their own words, usually restricted to 12 or fewer words, about the main idea of that section (approaches vary in terms of whether this is written down, discussed within a cooperative learning group, etc.).

The intensity of main idea instruction may vary based on the needs of the students. Introduction may be provided in whole-class instruction or in a small group; the amount of practice and feedback may vary; and this skill may be taught within a suite of reading skills or as a stand-alone comprehension skill.

In a later section, we discuss specific differentiation for our three students. We return to the topic of main idea to illustrate how the variations just mentioned can be applied to provide individualized applications for each of the students.

Strategies for Answering Questions

In addition to teaching children how to construct meaning as they read, classroom time is also spent on helping children learn test-taking strategies. One approach is to teach children how to identify the types of questions used for classroom and state tests and how to support their choices.

Question–Answer Relationships Strategy, or QAR, was developed by Raphael (1986) to teach students how to identify four different types of questions, based on the type of information they must find to answer them:

- Right There: Students will find the answers to these literal questions "right there" in one sentence in the text. For example, *When was the Declaration of Independence signed?*

- Think and Search: Students must search in more than one place in the text and think about how to synthesize this information in order to answer the question. For example, *Were there any differences of opinion among the 13 colonies as they developed this document?*

- The Author and You: Students will not find all the information they need to answer this type of question in the text. Students must think what the author has written and associate this with what they have already learned and their own experiences. For example, *How was the French Revolution like the American Revolution?*

- On Your Own: Students will be able to answer these questions based on their own knowledge or experience. For example, *If you were alive at the time, would you have participated in the Boston Tea Party? Why or why not?*

General Adaptations to Classroom Comprehension Instruction

There are a variety of general adaptations that can benefit all students but that are particularly useful for students with reading disabilities. These include adjustments to the text content, performance requirements on the part of the student, pacing of the lesson, the manner in which instruction is organized, and the amount and type of multisensory reinforcement. Table 6.3 contains a list of adaptations that are commonly implemented across the spectrum of educational settings.

General Adaptations for Our Three Students

The following discussion of our three students illustrates how general adaptations might be made for each of them.

Billy

As discussed in previous chapters, Billy receives in-class support in the general education classroom. Billy reads the same texts as the class but benefits from some adjustments in performance requirements shown in Table 6.3, such as having access to audio books that the computer reads to him. This permits him to concentrate on comprehending the text without being distracted by his difficulties in decoding it. His in-class support teacher uses direct instruction to reinforce the classroom teacher's instruction of comprehension strategies, providing practice to mastery.

Table 6.3.   Common adaptations for students with reading disability

Content	Difficulty level of text
	Amount of text
	Familiarity of content
Performance requirements	Text read to student (by teacher or electronic source)
	Type of response—recognition response (pointing, matching), oral, written, word processing
	Scribe
	Vocabulary bank
	Cue card to prompt steps of strategy or response
Pacing	Number of new strategies introduced in lesson
	Number of times strategy practiced in lesson
	Number of times strategy reviewed after lesson
Instructional procedure	Direct instructions
	Modeling
	Guided feedback
	Fading of prompts
Multisensory reinforcement	Graphic organizer
	Pictures
	Video/DVD
	Dramatization
	Color coding
	Drawing
	Tracing
	Manipulatives

Jim

Jim is also placed in a general education classroom and does not receive in-class support. With his strong oral language and high level of intelligence, Jim requires very few of the instructional adaptations shown in Table 6.3 except for the use of graphic organizers or other types of visual aids. He is occasionally pulled in to the in-class support teacher's group if he exhibits difficulty with the content of a classroom text or in learning a particular comprehension strategy introduced by the classroom teacher.

Cindy

Cindy receives replacement reading/language arts instruction in a pull-out resource room and benefits from a number of the instructional adaptations shown in Table 6.3. In this setting, teachers are permitted to modify the curriculum in terms of content and pacing. Other general accommodations for Cindy include access to a scribe; texts read to her; use of audio books, graphic organizers, vocabulary banks, and direct instruction; and extensive use of multisensory strategies.

RESEARCH ON COMPREHENSION
DIFFICULTIES AND INTERVENTIONS
REPORTED FOR STUDENTS WITH READING DISABILITIES

Students with reading disabilities have been shown to have difficulty in many aspects of reading comprehension, beyond the expected problems caused by initial or ongoing word recognition problems. They differ from "good readers" in terms of their background knowledge (Gersten, Fuchs, Williams, & Baker, 2001); they may not have the needed background knowledge, may not automatically access it, or may access incorrect or unrelated information, which undermines their interpretation of text (Roberts, Torgesen, Boardman, & Scammacca, 2008). Students with reading disabilities have been reported to lack text processing skills, including finding the main idea, supporting details, and ignoring information that is not pertinent (Gajria, Jitendra, Sood, & Sacks, 2007). They may lack inference skills (Fritschman, Deshler, & Schumaker, 2007; Gajria et al., 2007; Gersten et al., 2001).

Students with reading disabilities may exhibit limited knowledge of narrative text structures (Gardill & Jitendra, 1999) or expository text structures (Wilder & Williams, 2001) and how to use this knowledge to store and retrieve content information (Gajria et al., 2007). They may have difficulty monitoring their comprehension and repairing comprehension breakdowns (Wilder & Williams, 2001); they may lack the necessary tools to identify and repair these breakdowns when they occur (Roberts et al., 2008).

Instructing students with reading disabilities on how to comprehend text has been largely geared to teaching them how to apply strategies that good readers use. The research indicates that students with reading difficulties can learn these strategies and thus improve their comprehension, but will need more extensive, structured, and direct instruction than students with no reading disabilities to do so (Wilder & Williams, 2001). Mastropieri, Scruggs, and Graetz (2003) reported that effective interventions include strategy instruction and direct instruction using guided and independent practice. Outcomes are enhanced by including the greatest number of effective instructional components, that is, features such as one-to-one instruction, controlled difficulty of tasks, and supplementing teacher instruction with parents or homework. Gajria et al. (2007) reported positive findings for studies of cognitive strategies in which students learn how to learn, including teaching students to recognize types of text structure (e.g., comparison, cause–effect), to construct cognitive maps (e.g., Venn diagrams), generate self-questioning, identify main ideas or generate main idea sentences by paraphrasing or summarizing the reading passages. They reported that interventions incorporating complex strategies, with multiple components, such as reciprocal teaching were more effective than single strategy approaches (Gajria et al.).

Although the literature has generally demonstrated that strategy instruction is effective in teaching students with reading disabilities how to comprehend text, findings from a study with a low-performing general classroom population suggest that a content-oriented approach may be effective. McKeown, Beck, and Blake (2009) conducted a study in which they compared the effectiveness of the strategies approach to a content approach based on the Questioning the Author technique (Beck & McKeown, 2006). In content instruction, students were taught to attend to the text through questions. Teachers had students stop reading at purposely selected points in the text and asked a question to initiate discussions, for example, *"What's going on here?"* or *"How does all this connect with what we read earlier?"* Results indicated that on the more rigorous measures of comprehension, content students outperformed strategic students.

Visual aids, such as graphic organizers, have been shown to be "content enhancements" that are effective in teaching comprehension strategies to students with reading disabilities (Gardill & Jitendra, 1999; Kim, Vaughn, Wanzek, & Wei, 2004). Gajria et al. (2007) indicated that content enhancement is particularly helpful for students with reading disabilities by making difficult material more concrete and easier to remember. Boyle and Weishaar (1997) reported that students who develop their own organizers or who used expert-generated organizers demonstrated significantly higher scores than control group students, with students in the group that generated their own organizers performing better on measures of both literal and inferential comprehension. Computer software, such as Inspiration, that permits students to easily construct graphic organizers can be helpful (Mastropieri, Scruggs, Abdulrahman, and Gardizi, 2002).

Direct instruction in comprehension monitoring strategies has been shown to be effective for students with reading disabilities. These strategies include noting confusing or difficult words and concepts, creating images, and stopping after each paragraph to summarize (Roberts et al., 2008).

FORMAL AND INFORMAL ASSESSMENT OF LISTENING AND READING COMPREHENSION AND A PROCESS FOR COMBINING RESULTS TO IDENTIFY INDIVIDUAL STUDENTS' COMPREHENSION NEEDS

The types of general adaptations discussed previously are extremely helpful for enhancing comprehension instruction for students with reading disabilities. However, individual students' comprehension needs are best met by a finer differentiation of instruction that involves identifying the specific comprehension skills on which they need to work (i.e., the content of instruction), as well as the most suitable instructional approaches (i.e., the process of instruction). In order for teachers to differentiate comprehension instruction to this extent, it is necessary for them to have comprehensive data from formal and informal assessment, indicating students' reading comprehension needs *and* their oral language and cognitive strengths and weaknesses. In this section, we discuss the types of formal tests frequently used, discuss a kit of informal tests that teachers can use to identify weaknesses in specific comprehension skills (Appendix B), and present a system for consolidating data as a basis for instructional planning.

Formal Tests

There are a limited number of comprehension tests in frequent use. Tests vary in the manner in which they assess comprehension, and this might result in differences in results for an individual child. Table 6.4 lists the major tests used to assess reading comprehension.

Informal Assessment

While formal tests yield information on overall levels of comprehension, the information is not broken down for the teacher in a way that lends itself to instructional planning. We recommend that teachers augment results of formal testing by administering a kit of informal measures (Appendix B) based on selections of texts from their own classrooms—a type of curriculum-

Table 6.4. Formal reading comprehension tests

Test	Format	Type of response	Companion listening test
Woodcock-Johnson III (WJIII) Passage Comprehension	Cloze	Student reads silently, and then provides word missing in text.	Yes, identical format
Woodcock-Johnson Reading Mastery	Cloze	Student reads silently, and then provides word missing in text.	Yes, identical format
Wechsler Individual Achievement Test–II (WIAT-III) Reading Comprehension	Mix of narrative and expository passages within grade range, approximately one page in length	Student reads silently or aloud and then responds to questions asked by examiner; look backs allowed.	Yes, different format
Gray Oral Reading Test–4 (GORT-4)	Graded passages, one paragraph in length	Student reads orally, and then answers multiple-choice questions; no look backs allowed.	No
Gray Silent Reading Test (GSRT)	Graded passages, one paragraph in length	Student reads silently, and then answers multiple-choice questions; look backs allowed.	No
Test of Reading Comprehen-sion–4 (TORC-4)	Short passages, one paragraph in length	Student reads silently and then answers multiple-choice questions; look backs allowed.	No

based assessment. Three simple measures to start with, most of which can be done in a group, are

- Students' self-assessment of the strategies they use while reading

- Assessment of students' knowledge of story elements, obtained by having them complete a story map after reading a short narrative

- Assessment of students' reading comprehension of both narrative and expository text, obtained by having them answer literal and inferential questions after reading selections from classroom materials

In many school districts, some of the information above is obtained through a developmental reading assessment approach. In addition, some school districts have begun to administer criterion-referenced tests—usually at the beginning and the end of the school year—which yield results of student performance on specific comprehension skills, linked to state curriculum standards. These results may provide some of the information teachers need for instructional planning.

The Comprehension Needs Chart

Given the wealth of student data available on comprehension skills and related factors, it is helpful for teachers to integrate information from a variety of assessment sources into one system. Figure 6.1 presents the comprehension needs chart that we propose teachers use to consolidate student data. The chart permits teachers to enter data in categories pertinent to instructional planning, including the student's performance level on specific comprehension skills *that drive the "what" of instruction* and information on learner characteristics *that guide the "how" of instruction.* This chart helps teachers design the best approach to comprehension given a student's particular language and cognitive profile. The chart enables them to identify the specific comprehension skills that need attention and the oral language skills that support or undermine comprehension. Later in this chapter, we refer to this chart to plan instruction for our three students. Appendix C contains brief descriptions of each of the categories listed in the comprehension needs chart.

Using the comprehension needs chart, teachers translate results from formal and informal measures into one simple rating system for identifying instructional priorities. The following guidelines indicate how ratings are established for formal test results.

1   Needs substantial improvement   Below 35th percentile

2   Needs improvement   35th percentile–49th percentile

3   Adequate or better performance   50th percentile–65th percentile

To illustrate, for students with average cognitive ability, performance on formal tests is rated as 1 (Needs substantial improvement) when a score is below the 25th percentile. For example, Billy's teacher rates overall reading comprehension as a 2 (Needs improvement) based on the CST report of Billy performing at the 35th percentile on the Woodcock-Johnson III Passage Comprehension Subtest. Billy's receptive vocabulary as measured by the Peabody Picture Vocabulary Test was at the 40th percentile, and therefore that

Student: _____   Teacher: _____

Rate each item on the following scale:
1   Needs substantial improvement
2   Needs improvement
3   Adequate performance or better

Date: _____	Rating
LEARNER CHARACTERISTICS	
Verbal reasoning	
Receptive vocabulary	
Expressive vocabulary	
Listening comprehension	
Fluency	
Word attack	
Word identification	
Phonemic awareness	
Visual spatial	
Engagement	
Attention	
Working memory	
Background knowledge	
DATA ON WHAT TO TEACH	
Overall Reading Comprehension (formal)	
Overall Narrative	
Literal	
Inferential	
Overall Expository	
Literal	
Inferential	
Narrative and Expository: Before-Reading Strategies	
Access background knowledge	
Determine purpose for reading	
Preview text	
Make predictions	
Revise predictions as needed	
Narrative: During-Reading Strategies	
Recognize key information (setting, characters)	
Understand sequence	
Understand conflict	
Retell	
Summarize	
Understand emotions, beliefs	
Understand genre	
Understand recurring themes	

	Rating
Expository: During Reading Strategies	
Identify main idea	
Locate details	
Retell	
Summarize	
Recognize and understand description	
Recognize and understand sequence	
Recognize and understand classification	
Recognize and understand compare/contrast	
Recognize and understand cause and effect	
Narrative and Expository: After-Reading Strategies	
Make connection to prior knowledge	
Make inferences	
Generate explanations that extend text information	
Establish an opinion connected to text	
Metacognitive Skills	
Know strategies	
Vary strategies according to purpose of reading and nature of text	
Recognize comprehension breakdown	
Repair comprehension breakdown	
VISUAL AIDS	
Develop and use graphic organizers	
Recognize common organizational patterns that support comprehension (headings, caption)	

Figure 6.1.   Comprehension needs chart.

Ready to Read: A Multisensory Approach to Language-Based Comprehension Instruction by
Mary Lupiani Farrell, Ph.D. and Francie M. Matthews, Ph.D. Copyright © 2010 by
Paul H. Brookes Publishing Co., Inc. All rights reserved.

factor is rated as a 2. But, Billy performed below the 35th percentile on two measures of expressive language (WISC-IV Verbal Comprehension Index and WISC-IV Vocabulary Subtest) and that factor is rated 1.

A number of types of informal tests may be used to augment diagnostic information. Sample informal tests are given in Appendix B, including student's self-rating on use of comprehension strategies, protocols for assessing literal and inferential comprehension of expository and narrative texts, and a graphic organizer for assessing understanding of narrative components. Guidelines for assigning ratings depend on the nature of the test. For example, student's self-ratings on their use of comprehension strategies can initially be taken at face value and adjusted by teacher observation and follow-up informal assessment as needed. The Appendix B protocol for assessing narrative and expository passages suggests asking 5 literal and 5 inferential questions for each type of text. On this type of task, students are rated as 1 (Needs substantial improvement) if fewer than half of the items are correct. A review of the graphic organizer for narratives provides teachers with a basis for rating students on their understanding of story elements, such as setting and conflict.

Figure 6.2 reflects the ratings assigned for Billy's performance on the informal assessments provided in Appendix B. For example, because Billy got less than half of the inferential questions correct on the informal narrative comprehension measure, his teacher rated him as 1 (Needs substantial improvement); he earned the same rating on the inferential questions for the expository text. These ratings are used to complete the comprehension

Measure	# Correct/ percentile	Rating
• **Overall Comprehension Strategies (self-rating)**		
• Accesses background information		1
• Thinks about purpose for reading		2
• Previews text		2
• Makes predictions		1
• Adjusts predictions during reading		1
• Recognizes comprehension breakdown		2
• Repairs comprehension breakdown		1
• Makes connections to prior knowledge		1
• **Informal Narrative: Literal**	4/5	3
• **Informal Narrative: Inferential**	2/5	1
• **Informal Narrative: Graphic Organizer**		
• Identifies key information (character, setting, etc.)		3
• Identifies sequence		3
• Identifies conflict		3
• **Informal Expository: Literal**	4/5	2
• **Informal Expository: Inferential**	2/5	1
• **Main Idea**	1/2	2

Figure 6.2.   Billy's ratings on informal comprehension assessments.

needs chart. Any items not directly assessed in the comprehension needs chart can be rated on the basis of teacher observation of classroom performance over time.

Figure 6.3 presents Billy's comprehension needs chart, with ratings assigned by his teacher and based on the results of both formal and informal tests. Relative strengths and weaknesses are quickly and easily identified using the chart. As stated, the strengths/weaknesses may then be used as a basis for determining both the *process* and the *content* of comprehension instruction. Using Billy as an example to start, we illustrate how teachers can use this tool to consolidate information and plan individualized reading comprehension instruction.

DIFFERENTIAL APPLICATION OF TREATMENT STRATEGIES TO STUDENTS: OUR THREE STUDENTS

Billy

Looking over the ratings in the comprehension needs chart, it appears that relatively weak oral vocabulary, verbal reasoning, and working memory undermine Billy's comprehension ability. Although receptive vocabulary was rated as a 2, the teacher has noticed that Billy's word meanings can be quite shallow, and she plans to take this into consideration when planning instruction. Given the rating of 1 on verbal reasoning, the teacher concludes that Billy's weak inferential comprehension skills likely stem from his underdeveloped abstract thinking, and she plans to adapt her instructional approach accordingly. Poor working memory also seems to contribute to Billy's difficulties; it prevents him from keeping an adequate amount of information in mind at one time. The teacher decides to teach Billy compensatory strategies for his weak working memory. A strength for Billy is his visual-spatial ability. This suggests that he will respond well to graphic organizers. The teacher takes all of these factors into account in planning *how* to teach. The *content* of instruction will be prioritized using the ratings in the comprehension needs chart as a guide.

Because Billy is placed in a general education classroom, his comprehension instruction is not individualized, except for when he receives in-class support. The in-class support teacher selects the following areas to work on with Billy:

- Improve inferential skills, in particular
  - Identifying and expressing the main idea
  - Understanding characters' feelings
  - Making predictions
- Develop strategies for use before, during, and after reading
  - Accessing background information
  - Predictions
- Introduce QAR for test taking

Student: <u>Billy</u>   Teacher: <u>Ms. Adams</u>

Rate each item on the following scale:

1   Needs substantial improvement

2   Needs improvement

3   Adequate or better performance

Date: October 2, 2009	Rating		Rating
LEARNER CHARACTERISTICS		**Expository: During Reading Strategies**	
Verbal reasoning	1	Identify main idea	1
Receptive vocabulary	2	Locate details	2
Expressive vocabulary	1	Retell	1
Listening comprehension	2	Summarize	1
Fluency	1	Recognize and understand description	TBO
Word attack	1	Recognize and understand sequence	TBO
Word identification	1	Recognize and understand sequence	TBO
Phonemic awareness	1	Recognize and understand classification	TBO
Visual spatial	3	Recognize and understand classification	TBO
Engagement	3	Recognize and understand compare/contrast	TBO
Attention	3	Recognize and understand compare/contrast	TBO
Working memory	1	Recognize and understand cause and effect	TBO
Background knowledge	2	Recognize and understand cause and effect	TBO
DATA ON WHAT TO TEACH		**Narrative and Expository: After-Reading Strategies**	
Overall Reading Comprehension (formal)	2	Make connection to prior knowledge	1
Overall Narrative		Make connection to prior knowledge	1
Literal	2	Make inferences	1
Inferential	1	Generate explanations that extend text information	1
Overall Expository		Generate explanations that extend text information	1
Literal	2	Establish an opinion connected to text	2
Inferential	1	Establish an opinion connected to text	2
Narrative and Expository: Before-Reading Strategies		**Metacognitive Skills**	
Access background knowledge	1	Know strategies	1
Determine purpose for reading	2	Vary strategies according to purpose of reading and nature of text	1
Preview text	2	Vary strategies according to purpose of reading and nature of text	1
Make predictions	1	Vary strategies according to purpose of reading and nature of text	1
Revise predictions as needed	1	Recognize comprehension breakdown	2
Narrative: During-Reading Strategies		Recognize comprehension breakdown	2
Recognize key information (setting, characters)	3	Repair comprehension breakdown	1
Understand sequence	3	**VISUAL AIDS**	
Understand conflict	3	Develop and use graphic organizers	2
Retell	2	Develop and use graphic organizers	2
Summarize	1	Recognize common organizational patterns that support comprehension (headings, caption)	2
Understand emotions, beliefs	1	Recognize common organizational patterns that support comprehension (headings, caption)	2
Understand genre	TBO*	*TBO = to be observed	
Understand recurring themes	TBO		

Figure 6.3.   Billy's comprehension needs chart.

Billy's in-class support teacher designs the following approach based on data in the comprehension needs chart and observation of Billy's performance in class:

- Because of his difficulty with verbal reasoning, introduce content with experiences and examples Billy can relate to before requiring abstract thinking.

- Because of vocabulary weaknesses, carefully consider the language in texts and instruction.

- To compensate for poor working memory and vocabulary weaknesses, provide visual aids such as graphic organizers and pictures whenever possible. These tools will promote visualization of concepts as well.

Strategies for Improving Inference: Main Idea

Billy's in-class support teacher decides to teach the concept of main idea with expository text since comprehension of expository text has been shown to be more challenging for students than comprehension of narrative text. Moreover, a frequent assignment in Billy's social studies class is to identify the main idea of textbook sections. Billy's in-class teacher chooses the Getting the Gist strategy for teaching main idea, developed by Klinger, Vaughn, and Schumm (1998). Students are taught to follow the steps listed here:

- Read through the passage two paragraphs at a time.

- Determine whether what was read is mostly about a person, place, or a thing and specifically identify that subject.

- Identify the most important point about the subject.

- Write one sentence, comprising 12 words or less, that summarizes the most important point.

The teacher provides additional instructional sessions on this skill until Billy reaches mastery and then monitors his application of it on other assignments for an extended period of time.

Strategies for Improving Inference: Understanding Characters' Feelings

Billy's in-class support teacher notes that, on the informal narrative test, Billy showed adequate skills for the literal aspects of story comprehension, such as identifying setting and problem. However, his responses reflected a lack of higher level skills such as understanding characters' emotions and general themes. This finding was consistent with his language profile that indicated weaknesses in verbal reasoning. She adopts the following plan:

- Beginning at a fairly concrete level, the in-class support teacher models by thinking out loud how she would feel in the same situation as that presented in the story. She elicits from Billy how he would feel in a related situation with which he would be familiar.

- Continuing with a concrete approach, she lists the types of text (e.g., dialogue) in which he might find clues about a character's feelings, and she models how to identify these in text.

- Next, she guides him, providing feedback as they go, as he reads the next section of text and talks about the characters' feelings.

Strategies for Activating Background Knowledge Before, During and After Reading

The classroom teacher generally spends time helping the children activate their background knowledge related to the text; she also provides new background information. The in-class support teacher realizes that due to his language and working memory weaknesses, Billy is not absorbing the new information as easily as his classmates, and he needs reinforcement through repetition, using the following instructional strategies:

- She has observed that Billy benefits from having new material presented visually, and she uses pictures from the Internet to illustrate events discussed by the teacher.

- She asks eliciting questions to prompt Billy to think about his prior knowledge on the subject and to make connections between the pictures and the information which the teacher presented.

- The in-class support teacher models and then oversees Billy's use of the KWL graphic organizer for consolidating background information related to the text they are reading.

Before Reading: Making Predictions

The in-class support teacher, reviewing Billy's chart, decides that a critical "before-reading" skill to work on is making predictions. She gives him explicit instruction in making predictions, using a record-keeping form to make the approach concrete for Billy (Figure 6.4).

- Given the length of the chapter and her observation of the length of text to which Billy can profitably attend, she decides that he should reevaluate his predictions after each page and fill in the blank in the directions line accordingly.

- They discuss the title of the story and background information.

Initial Prediction: _____		
Pages	Check if Your Prediction Was Correct	Next Prediction

Figure 6.4. Prediction chart

- She models by thinking aloud and then writing on the record-keeping form her own brief prediction about what the story will be about.

- They read one page and the in-class support teacher models, again by thinking aloud, how to check the initial prediction by locating supporting information in the text. If her prediction was correct, she simply checks the second box on the form. If her prediction was not validated, she discusses why, citing specific information from the text, and then writes the revised prediction in the second box.

- She has Billy make a prediction for the next page and write that in the first box of the next row. She reads the next page with Billy and guides him in his thinking aloud about the prediction. She asks him to identify the place in the text where he can assess and prove or disprove his prediction. She oversees his completion of the record-keeping form.

- When the in-class support teacher is satisfied that Billy has mastered the process, she permits him to practice working on this activity independently in the classroom.

- If his independent classroom work is done satisfactorily, he may get an assignment to complete the chapter for homework.

Strategies for Introducing QAR

In addition to providing instruction for his *individualized* content needs, the in-class support teacher allocates some time to support the QAR strategy taught by the general education teacher. She develops a multisensory approach in which Billy learns to identify the various types of questions through systematic instruction in constructing his own questions.

In keeping with the principles of direct instruction, instruction begins with the simplest type of question, which Billy practices until it is mastered. To keep Billy's concentration on the task of generating questions and to get maximum exposure to the conceptual level of classroom texts, the teacher reads the classroom text with Billy rather than having him read it on his own.

The instructional process goes through the cycle below as Billy learns to master each of the four question types:

- Generate and answer a Right There question. The teacher models how to ask what, when, or how something is happening in a segment of text. She then requires Billy to formulate the questions, first orally and then in writing. Following successful question writing, Billy's teacher provides Right There questions from his classroom text for him to read and answer. She repeats this cycle for each of the question types.

  - Think and Search question

  - Author and You question

  - On Your Own question

Jim

Jim's oral language skills are excellent and greatly support his reading comprehension. He also has many other strong learner characteristics that help comprehension, such as expansive background knowledge. While most comprehension skills were given high ratings in the comprehension needs chart, a few areas received ratings of 2, for example, his understanding of cause and effect in expository texts and his ability to summarize what he reads. Jim seemed to need strategies for these comprehension skills. This data, along with the tutor's ongoing observations of Jim's ability to handle his school assignments, led her to work on the following areas with Jim:

- Understanding cause–effect text structure

- Summarization

The tutor makes the following process decisions:

- Because Jim's visual-spatial skills are excellent, she uses graphic organizers.

- She uses a learning strategies approach that gives Jim stepwise strategies. She sometimes provides a mnemonic to help him remember the steps.

- She promotes independent application of strategies by giving Jim check-lists and cues cards.

Strategies to Improve Understanding of Cause–Effect Text Structure

The tutor notes that when she is reading with Jim from his social studies text, he does not always pick up on cause–effect relationships, especially when there is more than one cause or effect in a passage. She discusses this observation with Jim's teacher; together, they develop a strategy to improve the ability to understand and describe cause and effect, which the teacher teaches in the context of social studies:

- The teacher discusses the idea that much of social studies involves cause–effect relationships and cites oral examples of such relationships recently studied.

- The teacher posts on the board a list of words that signal cause and effect and provides students with a personal list.

- The teacher presents a graphic organizer on the SMART Board with spaces to write causes on the left and effects on the right.

- The teacher reads a section of the text aloud with the class, locates signal words with them that signal the cause–effect relationship in the text, and then completes the graphic organizer with the class.

- The process is repeated with ensuing sections of text until the teacher ascertains that most of the class understands the concept.

- At this point, the teacher instructs the students to complete the remaining sections independently on their own graphic organizers.

Strategies to Improve Summarization

Initially Jim did not know how to identify the main idea. Instead, he gave all the details. From classroom instruction on Getting the Gist, he became proficient at expressing main ideas for a limited amount of text. While many students would automatically transfer this skill to summarization, Jim had trouble building on the main idea strategy to summarize longer amounts of text. Once again, he tended to tell *everything*, rather than just the main ideas. An ongoing assignment in language arts was to summarize each chapter of the novel the class was reading. To help him with summarization, his tutor gave him the following strategy as a structure for organizing his thoughts:

- Stop reading after every page and write down 1–2 words that tell what the page is mostly about.

- At the end of the chapter, look over the words and group those that are about the same idea.

- To write the summary, use a topic sentence starting with *This chapter is about* or *In this chapter.*

- Write one sentence about each group of words.

Cindy

As mentioned in Chapter 1, Cindy is in a pull-out replacement resource room with an individualized reading program. Her substantial oral language problems undermine her ability to comprehend written text. Her language profile will need to be kept in mind when choosing/adapting instructional approaches. Remedial work on the various language skill areas as described in previous chapters will be part of her overall comprehension program. Cindy needs instruction on almost every comprehension skill, but the teacher decides to begin with those she considers most basic:

- Improve ability to understand main idea in narrative and expository text

- Improve ability to recognize description

- Improve retelling ability

Strategies to Improve the Ability to
Understand Main Idea: Narrative and then Expository

Instruction for Cindy on an inferential skill such as main idea is best approached incrementally and concretely. Following is a sequence of instruction, adapted from Carnine et al. (1990), but moving from personal experiences, to narrative texts with and without pictures, to illustrated expository texts, to unillustrated expository texts. To control for content and background knowledge, the teacher selects a social studies topic (e.g., Civil War) on which both narrative and expository text can be found at the level of Cindy's listening comprehension ability. For reinforcement, follow-up practice is given with material at Cindy's reading level, and the strategy is regularly practiced in classroom materials. Cindy's teacher begins with the first step and repeats each step until mastered before proceeding to the next step. The teacher models, scaffolds, and guides instruction throughout.

STEP 1: Find the main idea in personal experience, based on sets of photographs.

- Cindy identifies the main idea of pictures that involve a single subject. For example, the teacher presents photographs from Cindy's birthday party; Cindy identifies the subject and what is happening.

- Cindy identifies the main idea in pictures that involve a group. For example, the teacher presents photographs of Cindy's class in physical education; Cindy identifies the subjects and what they are doing.

STEP 2: Find the main idea in narrative text, or a picture book if necessary, ideally on the same subject as the subject of expository text.

- Cindy identifies the main idea of a picture book story that involves a single subject, for example, a young drummer boy in the Civil War. For multisensory reinforcement, Cindy draws a picture of the young drummer boy and what he is doing.

- Cindy identifies the main idea of narrative text that involves more than one subject, for example, the young drummer boy and the rest of the fife and drum corps. For multisensory reinforcement, Cindy tells a brief story about a group she knows, for example, her brownie troop and how they made s'mores.

- Cindy identifies the main idea when a concept—as opposed to a person or people—is the subject. The teacher presents a narrative passage about when something happened, how something is done, or how something looks. Three possible main ideas are presented. Cindy looks at each main idea option and checks how many sentences refer to that option. If most of the sentences are about a particular main idea option, then that is the main idea. Multiple-choice responses provide structure for her in this more abstract thinking.

- When Cindy is successful in selecting the main idea from multiple choice exercises, she reads subsequent sections of text and expresses the main idea orally.

STEP 3: Find the main idea in expository text, using illustrated text first and then progressing to text without pictures.

- Using a passage about one person only, Cindy identifies the subject of the text and what the person is doing.

- Using a passage about more than one person, Cindy identifies the subjects and what they are doing.

- Using a passage about something that happened, Cindy tells what happened.

STEP 4: Practice finding main idea throughout subject areas and use main idea skill series for additional practice.

Strategies for Recognizing Description

- Begin by presenting Cindy with the simple text.

- Use a scaffolding approach that includes modeling, thinking aloud, asking eliciting questions, giving multisensory cues, and guided feedback.

- Read descriptive text with Cindy.

- Stop after a short section and discuss the picture that the author paints with his or her words. Ask Cindy to draw that picture, with the teacher modeling that activity as needed. Help Cindy interpret the description, by asking eliciting questions that help her focus in on the information provided. For example, "What might you be hearing in this scene?"

- When Cindy is successful at visualizing descriptions the teacher provides, have Cindy find descriptive passages on her own and describe the picture that the author presents.

Strategies for Retelling

- Begin the instruction by describing a personal experience (e.g., a weekend activity).

- Provide a story frame with visual prompts for Cindy to use to organize her thoughts prior to retelling.

- Use a scaffolding approach: model how to use the graphic organizer; guide Cindy through the process of completing the organizer by eliciting questions and feedback; gradually diminish the level of support.

- Scribe for Cindy throughout the process.

- Have Cindy retell the narrative by using the graphic aid, with prompting as needed.

- Organize instruction to go from retelling the personal experience to reading and retelling a simple, structured story with a clear main character, to stories with more than one character or problem. The story is either at Cindy's readability level or the teacher reads it to her.

SUMMARY

Listening comprehension forms the basis for reading comprehension. However, the processes involved in the two types of comprehension are not identical. Listening comprehension is initially better than reading comprehension. The difference in students' ability in the two different types of comprehension decreases beginning in Grade 2 for readers with no learning disabilities. Children's reading comprehension abilities advance when their basic reading skills become automatic and they become less glued to the text. At this point children begin to read to learn. Reading strategies commonly taught in mainstream classes include DRTA, KWL, and QAR, as well as techniques for identifying the main idea. A number of general adaptations, commonly implemented by practitioners, may be used to enhance success for students with reading disabilities in reading comprehension instruction. Research has shown that students with reading disabilities may have difficulties with various aspects of reading comprehension including use of background knowledge, text processing, inference, knowledge of text structure, and monitoring and repairing comprehension breakdowns. Strategy instruction and direct instruction using guided and independent practice, content-oriented instruction, and instruction in the use of visual aids, such as graphic organizers, have all been shown to be effective in improving students' reading comprehension skills. A comprehension needs chart was presented as a tool through which teachers can integrate information on oral language and other pertinent factors to plan individualized reading comprehension instruction. Goals for our three students as well as related individualized interventions were presented as examples.

CONCLUSION

Three subtypes of students with reading disabilities, distinguished by their oral language profiles, have been presented. Jim, Billy, and Cindy shared early problems in phonological processing, word recognition, and fluency. They differed significantly, however, in oral language abilities and consequently in comprehension. Jim, with pure dyslexia, had strong oral language abilities and was able to draw upon these skills to help compensate for his reading disorder. Billy had a mixed reading disability stemming from both dyslexia and mild language problems and benefitted from comprehension adapted to meet these needs. Cindy, a student with specific language impairment, experienced a range of oral language, which undermined her development of upper level reading skills. She required consistent and intensive intervention in both oral and written language.

Readers might wonder what happened to our students. Jim, with a 504 Plan and tutoring when needed, successfully completed middle school and high school. Building on his spatial strengths, he pursued an architectural major in college. Billy successfully completed middle school and high school with the help of in-class support. Given his outstanding performance in several varsity level sports, he was recruited with an athletic scholarship by a state university and majored in education. Cindy flourished in the small private school for students with learning disabilities. She attended a college with a comprehensive support program for her learning disabilities. Taking a minimum full-time load each semester, she graduated with a degree in merchandizing in 5 years.

All three students received 504 accommodations at the college level to compensate for residual problems with reading rate and spelling. The prescriptive instruction they received early on helped them become the successful people they are today: architect, teacher/football coach, and boutique owner.

References

Adams, M.J., Foorman, B.R., Lundberg, I., & Beeler, T. (1998). *Phonemic awareness in young children: A classroom curriculum.* Baltimore: Paul H. Brookes Publishing Co.

Americans with Disabilities Act Amendments Act of 2008, PL 110-325, § 3406

Anderson, R.C., & Freebody, P. (1981). Vocabulary knowledge. In J.T. Guthrie (Ed.), *Comprehension and teaching: Research review* (pp. 71–117). Newark, DE: International Reading Association.

Anglin, J.M., Miller, G.A., & Wakefield, P.C. (1993). Vocabulary development: A morphological analysis. *Monographs of the Society for Research in Child Development, 58*(10), 150–177.

Beck, I.L., & McKeown, M.G. (2006). *Improving comprehension with Questioning the Author: A fresh and expanded view of a powerful approach.* New York: Scholastic.

Beck, I.L., McKeown, M.G., & Kucan, L. (2002). *Bringing words to life: Robust vocabulary instruction.* London: Guilford Press.

Beck, I.L., McKeown, M.G., & Kucan, L. (2008). *Creating robust vocabulary.* New York: Guilford Press.

Beck, I.L., Perfetti, C.A., & McKeown, M. (1982). The effects of long-term vocabulary instruction on lexical access and reading comprehension. *Journal of Educational Psychology, 74*(4), 506–521.

Berninger, V.W., & Wolf, B.J. (2009). *Teaching students with dyslexia and dysgraphia: Lessons from teaching and science.* Baltimore: Paul H. Brookes Publishing Co.

Bishop, D.V.M., & Snowling, M.J. (2004). Developmental dyslexia and specific language impairment: Same or different? *Psychological Bulletin, 130,* 858–886.

Blachman, B.A. (1991). Getting ready to read: Learning how print maps to speech. In J.F. Kavanagh (Ed.), *The language continuum: From infancy to literacy* (pp. 41–62). Timonium, MD: York Press.

Bloom, L., & Lahey, M. (1978). *Language development and language disorders.* New York: Wiley & Sons, Inc.

Bowey, J.A. (1986). Syntactic awareness in relation to reading skill and ongoing reading comprehension monitoring. *Journal of Experimental Child Psychology, 41,* 282–99.

Boyle, J.R., & Weishaar, M. (1997). The effects of expert-generated versus student-generated cognitive organizers on the reading comprehension of students with learning disabilities. *Learning Disabilities Research & Practice, 12*(4), 228–235.

Brown, R. (1973). *A first language: The early stages.* Cambridge, MA: Harvard University Press.

Brown, V.L., Wiederholt, J.L., & Hammill, D.D. (2009). *Test of Reading Comprehension* (4th ed.). Austin, TX: PRO-ED.

Brownell, R. (2000). *Expressive and Receptive One-Word Picture Vocabulary Tests* (3rd ed.). Novato, CA: Academic Therapy Publication.

Bryant, D.O., Goodwin, M., Bryant, B.R., & Higgins, K. (2003). Vocabulary instruction for students with learning disabilities: A review of the literature. *Learning Disabilities Quarterly, 26,* 117–128.

Cain, K., & Oakhill, J. (2007). *Children's comprehension problems in oral and written language: A cognitive perspective.* New York: Guilford Press.

Carlisle, J.F. (1995). Morphological awareness and early reading achievement. In L.B. Feldman (Ed.), *Morphological aspects of language processing* (pp. 189–209). Hillsdale, NJ: Lawrence Erlbaum Associates.

Carlisle, J.F. (2000). Awareness of the structure and meaning of morphologically complex words: Impact on reading. *Reading and Writing, 12*(3–4), 169–190.

Carlisle, J.F., & Katz, L.A. (2005). Word learning and vocabulary instruction. In J.R. Birsh (Ed.), *Multisensory teaching of basic language skills* (2nd ed., pp. 345–375). Baltimore: Brookes Publishing Co.

Carlisle, J.F., & Nomanbhoy, D. (1993). Phonological and morphological development. *Applied Psycholinguistics, 14,* 177–195.

Carlisle, J.F., & Rice, M.S. (2002). *Improving reading comprehension: Research-based principles and practices.* Baltimore: York Press.

Carlisle, J.F., & Stone, C.A. (2003). The effects of morphological structure on children's reading of derived words. In E. Assink & D. Santa (Eds.), *Reading complex words: Cross-language studies* (pp. 27–52). New York: Kluwer Academic.

Carnine, D., Silbert, J., & Kameenui, E. (1990). *Direct instruction reading* (2nd ed.). Columbus, OH: Merrill.

Carnine, D.W., Silbert, J., Kameenui, E.J., Tarver, S.G., & Jungjohann, K. (2006). *Teaching struggling and at-risk readers: A direct instruction approach.* Upper Saddle River, NJ: Pearson.

Carrow-Woolfolk, E. (1999). *Comprehensive Assessment of Spoken Language.* Circle Pines, MN: American Guidance Service.

Carrow-Woolfolk, E. (1999). *Test for Auditory Comprehension of Language–Third Edition (TACL-3).* Austin, TX: PRO-ED.

Casalis, S., Cole, P., & Sopo, D. (2004). Morphological awareness in developmental dyslexia. *Annals of Dyslexia, 54*(1), 114–138.

Catts, H., Adlof, S.M., Hogan, T.P., & Weismer, S.E. (2005). Are specific language impairment and dyslexia distinct disorders? *Journal of Speech, Language, and Hearing Research, 48,* 1378–1396.

Catts, H.W., Adlof, S.M., & Weismer, S.E. (2006). Language deficits in poor comprehenders: A case for the simple view of reading. *Journal of Speech, Language, and Hearing Research, 49,* 278–293.

Catts, H., & Kamhi, A. (2005). *Language and reading disabilities* (2nd ed.). Boston: Pearson.

Chall, J.S. (1983). *Stages of reading development.* New York: McGraw-Hill.

Cohen, V.L., & Cowen, J.E. (2008). *Literacy for children in an information age.* Belmont, CA: Thomson Wadsworth.

Cunningham, A.E. (2005). Vocabulary growth through independent reading and reading aloud to children. In E.H. Hiebert &

M.L. Kamil (Eds.), *Teaching and learning vocabulary: Bringing research to practice* (pp. 45–68). Mahwah, NJ: Lawrence Erlbaum Associates.

Dunn, L.M., & Dunn, D.M. (2007). *Peabody Picture Vocabulary Test* (4th ed.). Minneapolis, MN: Pearson.

Elbro, C., & Arnbak, E. (1996). The role of morpheme recognition and morphological awareness in dyslexia. *Annals of Dyslexia, 46,* 209–240.

Fiore, C., Boon, R.T., & Lowrie, K. (2007). Vocabulary instruction for middle school students with learning disabilities: A comparison of two instructional models. *Learning Disabilities: A Contemporary Journal 5*(2), 49–73.

Fritschmann, N.S., Deshler, D.D., & Schumaker, J.B. (2007). The effects of instruction in an inference strategy on the reading comprehension skills of adolescents with disabilities. *Learning Disabilities Quarterly, 30,* 245–262.

Gajria, M., Jitendra, A.K., Sood, S., & Sacks, G. (2007). Improving comprehension of expository text in students with LD: A research synthesis. *Journal of Learning Disabilities, 40,* 210–225.

Gardill, M.C., & Jitendra, A.K. (1999). Advanced story map instruction: Effects on the reading comprehension of students with learning disabilities. *Journal of Special Education, 33*(1), 2–17, 28.

Gersten, R., Fuchs, L.S., Williams, J.P., & Baker, S. (2001). Teaching reading comprehension strategies to students with learning disabilities: A review of research. *Review of Educational Research, 71*(2), 279–320.

Golinkoff, R., Hirsh-Pasek, K., Cauley, K., & Gordon, P. (1987). The eyes have it: Lexical and syntactic comprehension in a new paradigm. *Journal of Child Language, 14,* 23–46.

Halliday, M.A.K., & Hasan, R. (1976). *Cohesion in English.* London: Longman.

Hammill, D.D., Brown, V.L., Larsen, S.C., Wiederholt, J.L. (2007). *Test of Adolescent Language-4.* Austin, TX: PRO-ED.

Hammill, D.D., & Newcomer, P.L. (2008a). *Test of Language Development: Intermediate* (4th ed.). Austin, TX: PRO-ED.

Hammill, D.D., & Newcomer, P.L. (2008b). *Test of Language Development: Primary* (4th ed.). Austin, TX: PRO-ED.

Hiebert, E.H., & Kamil, M.L. (2005). *Teaching and learning vocabulary: Bringing research to practice.* Mahwah, NJ: Lawrence Erlbaum Associates.

Henry, M.K. (1988). Beyond phonics: Integrated decoding and spelling instruction based on word origin and structure. *Annals of Dyslexia, 38,* 259–275.

Henry, M.K. (1989). Children's word structure knowledge: Implications for decoding and spelling instruction. *Reading and Writing: An Interdisciplinary Journal, 2,* 135–152.

Henry, M.K. (2003). *Unlocking literacy: Effective decoding and spelling instruction.* Baltimore: Paul H. Brookes Publishing Co.

Hook, P.E., & Jones, S.D. (2002). The importance of automaticity and fluency for efficient reading comprehension. *Perspectives, 28,* 9–14.

Hughes, T.A., & Fredrick, L.D. (2006). Teaching vocabulary with students with learning disabilities using classwide peer tutoring and constant time delay. *Journal of Behavioral Education, 15*(1), 1–23.

Jitendra, A.K., Cole, C.L., Hoppes, M.K., & Wilson, B. (1998). Effects of a direct instruction main idea summarization program and self-monitoring on reading comprehension of middle school students with learning disabilities. *Reading & Writing Quarterly, 14*(4), 379–396.

Jitendra, A.K., Edwards, L.L., Sacks, G., & Jacobsen, L.A. (2004). What research says about vocabulary instruction for students with learning disabilities. *Exceptional Children, 70*(3), 299–322.

Kim, A., Vaughn, S., Wanzek, J., & Wei, S. (2004). Graphic organizers and their effects on the reading comprehension of students with LD: A synthesis of research. *Journal of Learning Disabilities, 37*(2), 105–118.

Klingner, J., Vaughn, S., & Boardman, A. (2007). *Teaching reading comprehension to students with learning difficulties.* New York: Guilford Press.

Klingner, J.K., Vaughn, S., & Schumm, J.S. (1998). Collaborative strategic reading during social studies in heterogeneous fourth-grade classrooms. *The Elementary School Journal, 99*(1), 3–23.

Lehr, F., Osborn, J., & Hiebert, E.H. (2004). *A focus on vocabulary (Research based practices in early reading series).* Honolulu, HI: Pacific Resources for Education and Learning.

Leonard, L.B. (1998). *Children with specific language impairment.* Cambridge, MA: The MIT Press.

Lyon, G.R., Shaywitz, S., & Shaywitz, B. (2003). A definition of dyslexia. *Annals of Dyslexia, 53,* 1–14.

Mastropieri, M.A., Scruggs, T.E., Abdulrahman, N., & Gardizi, W. (2002). *Computer assisted instruction in spatial organization strategies to facilitate high school content area learning.* Fairfax, VA: George Mason University, Graduate School of Education.

Mastropieri, M.A., Scruggs, T.E., & Graetz, J.E. (2003). Reading comprehension instruction for secondary students: Challenges for struggling students and teachers. *Learning Disabilities Quarterly, 26,* 103–116.

McGregor, K.K. (2004). Developmental dependencies between lexical semantics and reading. In C.A. Stone, E.R. Sillman, B.J. Ehren, & K. Apel (Eds.), *Handbook of language and literacy: development and disorders* (pp. 302–317). New York: Guilford Press.

McKeown, M.G., Beck, I.L., & Blake, R.G. (2009). Rethinking reading comprehension instruction: A comparison of instruction for strategies and content approaches. *Reading Research Quarterly, 44*(3), 218–253.

Metsala, J., & Walley, A. (1998). Spoken vocabulary growth and the segmental restructuring of lexical representations: Precursors to phonemic awareness and early reading ability. In J. Metsala & L. Ehri (Eds.), *Word recognition in beginning literacy* (pp. 89–120). Mahwah, NJ: Lawrence Erlbaum Associates.

Meyer, M.S., & Felton, R.H. (1999). Repeated reading to enhance fluency: old approaches and new directions. *Annals of Dyslexia, 49,* 283–306.

Moats, L.C., & Dakin, K.E. (2008). *Basic facts about dyslexia & other reading problems.* Baltimore: International Dyslexia Association.

Nagy, W.E., & Anderson, R.C. (1984). How many words in printed school English? *Reading Research Quarterly, 19,* 304–330.

Nation, K., & Snowling, M. (1998). Individual differences in contextual facilitation: Evidence from dyslexia and poor reading comprehension. *Child Development, 69,* 996–1011.

National Early Literacy Panel. (2008). *Developing early literacy: Report of the National Early Literacy Panel.* Washington, DC: National Institute for Literacy.

Neville, D.D., & Searls, E.F. (1985). The effect of sentence-combining and kernel-identification on the syntactic component of reading comprehension. *Research in the Teaching of English, 19,* 37–60.

Ogle, D.M. (1986). K-W-L: A teaching model that develops active reading of expository text. *The Reading Teacher, 39,* 564–570.

Pany, D., & Jenkins, J.R. (1978). Learning word meanings: A comparison of instructional procedures. *Learning Disability Quarterly, 1,* 21–32.

Pinkney, A.D. (2000). *Alvin Ailey.* Parsippany, NJ: Silver Burdett Ginn.

Raphael, T.E. (1986). Teaching question answer relationships, revisited. *The Reading Teacher, 39,* 516–522.

Reed, D.K. (2008). A synthesis of morphology interventions and effects on reading outcomes for students in grades K–12. *Learning Disabilities Research & Practice, 23*(1), 36–49.

Rice, M.L. (2003). A unified model of specific and general language delay: Grammatical tense as a clinical marker of unexpected variation. In Y. Levy & J. Schaeffer (Eds.), *Language competence across the populations: Towards a definition of specific language impairment* (pp. 209–231). Mahwah, NJ: Lawrence Erlbaum Associates.

Roberts, G., Torgesen, J.K., Boardman, A., & Scammacca, N. (2008). Evidence-based strategies for reading instruction of older students with learning disabilities. *Learning Disabilities Research & Practice, 23*(2), 63–69.

Roth, F.P., Speece, D.L., & Cooper, D.H. (2002). A longitudinal analysis of the connection between oral language and early reading. *Journal of Educational Research, 95,* 259–272.

Scarborough, H.S. (1990). Very early language deficits in dyslexic children. *Child Development, 61,* 1728–1743.

Scott, C. (1995). Syntax for school-age children: A discourse approach. In M. Fey, J. Windsor, & S. Warren (Eds.), *Language intervention: preschool through the elementary years* (pp. 107–143). Baltimore: Paul H. Brookes Publishing Co.

Scott, C.M. (2009). A case for the sentence in reading comprehension. *Language, Speech, and Hearing Services in Schools, 40,* 184–191.

Scott, C.M., & Windsor, J. (2000). General language performance measures in spoken and written narrative and expository discourse of school-age children with language learning disabilities. *Journal of Speech, Language and Hearing Research, 43,* 324–339.

Scruggs, T.E., Mastropieri, M.A., Bakken, J.P., & Brigham, F.J. (1993). Reading vs. doing: The relative effects of textbook-based and inquiry-oriented approaches to science learning in special classrooms. *Journal of Special Education, 27*(1), 1–15.

Seigneuric, A., & Ehrlich, M.F. (2005). Contribution of working memory capacity to children's reading comprehension: A longitudinal investigation. *Reading and Writing: An Interdisciplinary Journal, 18,* 617–656.

Semel, E., Wiig, E.H., & Secord, W.A. (2003). *Clinical Evaluation of Language Fundamentals* (4th ed.). San Antonio, TX: PsychCorp.

Shankweiler, D., Grain, S., Katz, L., Fowler, C., Liberman, A., Brady, S., et al. (1995). Cognitive profiles of reading-disabled children: Comparisons of language skills in phonology, morphology, and syntax. *Psychological Science, 6,* 149–156.

Shaywitz, S. (2003). *Overcoming dyslexia: A new and complete science-based program for dealing problems at any level.* New York: Alfred A. Knopf.

Silliman, E.R., & Scott, C.M. (2006). Language impairment and reading disability: Connections and complexities. Introduction to the special issue. *Learning Disabilities Research and Practice, 21*(1), 1–7.

Singson, M., Mahony, D., & Mann, V. (2000). Reading Ability and sensitivity to morphological relations. *Reading and Writing: An Interdisciplinary Journal, 12,* 191–218.

Soifer, L. (2005). Development of oral language and its relationship to literacy. In

J.R. Birsh (Ed.), *Multisensory teaching of basic language skills* (2nd ed., pp. 43–82). Baltimore: Paul H. Brookes Publishing Co.

Stanovich, K. (1986). Matthew effects in reading: Some consequences of individual differences in the acquisition of literacy. *Reading Research Quarterly, 21,* 360–407.

Stauffer, R.G. (1969). *Directing the reading-thinking process.* New York: Harper and Row.

Thompson, C., & Shapiro, L. (2007). Complexity in treatment of syntactic deficits. *American Journal of Speech-Language Pathology, 18,* 30–42.

Thorndike, R.L. (1973). *Reading comprehension education in fifteen countries* (International Studies in Evaluation III). Stockholm, Sweden: Almquist and Wiksell.

Tyler, A., & Nagy, W. (1990). Use of derivational morphology during reading. *Cognition, 36,* 17–34.

Vadasy, P.F., Sanders, E.A., & Peyton, J.A. (2006). Paraeducator-supplemented instruction in structural analysis with text reading practice for second and third graders at risk for reading problems. *Remedial and Special Education, 27*(6), 365–378.

Vaughn, S., & Klingner, J.K. (1999). Teaching reading comprehension through collaborative strategic reading. *Intervention in School & Clinic, 34*(5), 284–292.

Vogel, S.A. (1983). A qualitative analysis of morphological ability in learning disabled and achieving children. *Journal of Learning Disabilities, 16*(7), 416–420.

Wagner, R.K., Torgesen, J.K., & Rashotte, C. (1999). *Comprehensive Test of Phonological Processing (CTOPP).* Austin, TX: PRO-ED.

Wallach, G.P., & Miller, L. (1988). *Language intervention and academic success.* Austin, TX: PRO-ED.

Wechsler, D. (2009). *The Wechsler Individual Achievement Test—III.* San Antonio, TX: Pearson.

Wechsler, D. (2003). *The Wechsler Intelligence Scale for Children–Fourth Edition (WICS-IV).* San Antonio, TX: Pearson.

Wiederholt, J.L., & Bryant, B.R. (2001). *Gray Oral Reading Tests–Fourth Edition (GORT-4).* Austin, TX: PRO-ED.

Wiederholt, J.L., & Blalock, G. (2000). *Gray Silent Reading Tests (GSRT).* Austin, TX: PRO-ED.

Wilder, A.A., & Williams, J.P. (2001). Students with severe learning disabilities can learn higher order comprehension skills. *Journal of Educational Psychology, 93*(2), 268–278.

Wilkinson, P., & Patty, D. (1993). The effects of sentence combining on the reading comprehension of fourth grade students. *Research in the Teaching of English, 27,* 104–125.

Wolf, M., Miller, L., & Donnelly, K. (2000). Retrieval, automaticity, vocabulary elaboration, orthography (RAVE-O): Reading intervention program. *Journal of Learning Disability,* 375–386.

Woodcock, R.W., McGrew, K.S., & Mather, N. (2001). *Woodcock-Johnson III: Complete Battery.* Itasca, IL: Riverside.

Pertinent Formal Test Results

Pertinent Formal Test Results for Billy

Skill area	Formal test used	Standard score (SS)/percentile
IQ		
Full scale	Wechsler Intelligence Scale for Children–IV (WISC-IV)	98/47th
Oral language ability		
Mixed language skills	WISC-IV Verbal Comprehension Index	94/35th
Verbal reasoning	WISC-IV Similarities Subtest	8/25th
Receptive vocabulary	Peabody Picture Vocabulary Test	96/40th
Expressive vocabulary	WISC-IV Vocabulary Subtest	8/25th
Listening comprehension	Woodcock-Johnson Battery III (WJIII) Oral Comprehension Subtest	96/48th
Phonological awareness	Comprehensive Test of Phonological Processing (CTOPP) Phonological Awareness Scale	85/16th
Rapid naming	CTOPP Rapid Naming Scale	85/16th
Reading*		
Single-word reading	WJIII Letter-Word Identification Subtest	93/32nd
Nonsense word reading	WJIII Word Attack Subtest	90/25th
Reading fluency	WJIII Reading Fluency Subtest	85/16th
Reading comprehension	WJIII Passage Comprehension Subtest	94/35th
Other		
Working memory	WISC-IV Working Memory Index	79/21st
Spatial skills	WISC-IV Block Design Subtest	12/75th
Visual memory	WJIII Picture Recognition	100/50th
Processing speed	WISC-IV Processing Speed Index	104/60th

*Represents reading levels after 2 years of basic skills remediation

Pertinent Formal Test Results for Cindy

Skill area	Formal test used	Standard score (SS)/percentile
IQ		
Full Scale	Wechsler Intelligence Scale for Children—IV (WISC-IV)	94/35th
Oral language ability		
Mixed language skills	WISC-IV Verbal Comprehension Index	90/25th
Verbal reasoning	WISC-IV Similarities Subtest	7/16th
Receptive vocabulary	Receptive One-Word Picture Vocabulary Test	95/37th
Expressive vocabulary	Expressive One-Word Picture Vocabulary Test	88/21st
	WISC-IV Vocabulary Subtest	8/25th
Listening comprehension	Comprehensive Assessment of Spoken Language (CASL) Paragraph Assessment Subtest	85/16th
Morphosyntactic skills	CASL Grammaticality Judgment Subtest	82/12th
	Grammatical Morphemes Subtest	79/8th
Phonological awareness	Comprehensive Test of Phonological Processing (CTOPP) Phonological Awareness Scale	80/9th
Rapid naming ability	CTOPP Rapid Naming Scale	85/16th
Reading*		
Single-word reading	Woodcock-Johnson III (WJIII) Letter Word Identification Subtest	88/21st
Nonsense word reading	WJIII Word Attack Subtest	82/12th
Reading fluency	WJIII Reading Fluency Subtest	85/16th
Reading comprehension	WJIII Passage Comprehension Subtest	82/12th
Other		
Working memory	WISC-IV Working Memory Index	85/16th
Spatial skills	WISC-IV Block Design Subtest	11/63rd
Visual memory	WJIII Picture Recognition	100/50th
Processing speed	WISC-IV Processing Speed Index	100/50th

*Represents reading level after 2 years of basic skill remediation

Pertinent Formal Test Results for Jim

Skill area	Formal test used	Standard score (SS)/percentile
IQ		
Full scale	Wechsler Intelligence Scale for Children–IV (WISC-IV)	128/97th
Oral language ability		
Mixed language skills	WISC-IV Verbal Comprehension Index	130/98th
Verbal reasoning	WISC-IV Similarities Subtest	135/99th
Receptive vocabulary	No score	No score
Expressive vocabulary	WISC-IV Vocabulary Subtest	135/99th
Listening comprehension	Woodcock-Johnson Battery III (WJIII) Oral Comprehension Subtest	125/95th
Phonological awareness	Comprehensive Test of Phonological Processing (CTOPP) Phonological Awareness Scale	85/16th
Rapid naming	CTOPP Rapid Naming Scale	100/50th
Reading*		
Single-word reading	WJIII Letter-Word Identification Subtest	100/50th
Nonsense word reading	WJIII Word Attack Subtest	96/40th
Reading fluency	WJIII Reading Fluency Subtest	96/40th
Reading vocabulary	WJIII Reading Vocabulary Subtest	104/60th
Reading comprehension	WJIII Passage Comprehension Subtest	115/85th
Other		
Working memory	WISC-IV Working Memory Index	94/35th
Spatial skills	WISC-IV Block Design Subtest	119/90th
Visual memory	WJIII Picture Recognition	112/75th
Processing speed	WISC-IV Processing Speed Index	118/88th

*Reflects reading levels after 2 years of basic skills remediation

Informal Reading Comprehension Test

Self-Assessment of Reading Comprehension Strategies

Name: _____

Please circle the word that best explains how you read.

1. Before I read something, I think about information I already have on the topic.

    Never   Sometimes   Often   Never

2. Before I read something, I know why I am reading it.

    Never   Sometimes   Often   Never

3. Before I read something, I look ahead at pictures, titles, and headings.

    Never   Sometimes   Often   Never

4. Before I read something, I usually try to think what it will be about.

    Never   Sometimes   Often   Never

5. After I start reading, I change my mind about what I expect to happen in the reading.

    Never   Sometimes   Often   Never

Ready to Read: A Multisensory Approach to Language-Based Comprehension Instruction by
Mary Lupiani Farrell, Ph.D. and Francie M. Matthews, Ph.D. Copyright © 2010 by
Paul H. Brookes Publishing Co., Inc. All rights reserved.

6. If I don't understand what I am reading, I go back and read it again.

   Never   Sometimes   Often   Never

7. If I don't understand what I am reading, I read more slowly.

   Never   Sometimes   Often   Never

8. I think about what is the most important information while I am reading.

   Never   Sometimes   Often   Never

9. When I am finished reading, I think about what I already knew and the new information.

   Never   Sometimes   Often   Never

10. When I am finished reading, I have an opinion about what I read.

    Never   Sometimes   Often   Never

Ready to Read: A Multisensory Approach to Language-Based Comprehension Instruction by
Mary Lupiani Farrell, Ph.D. and Francie M. Matthews, Ph.D. Copyright © 2010 by
Paul H. Brookes Publishing Co., Inc. All rights reserved.

Story Map

This story map may be used to assess a student's mastery of narrative story elements. After the student has read or listened to a story, have him or her complete the story map. You may scribe for students who have difficulty completing the story map independently.

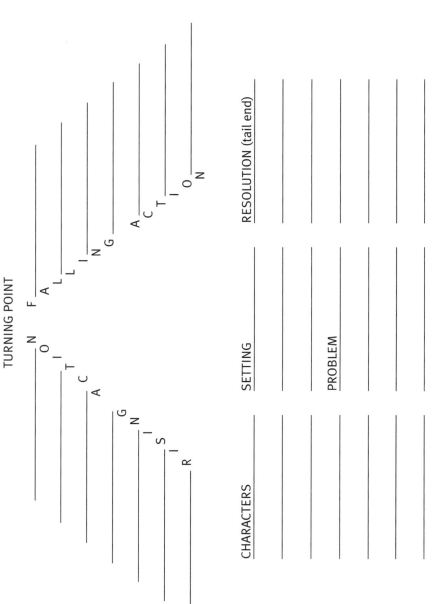

TURNING POINT

CHARACTERS

SETTING

PROBLEM

RESOLUTION (tail end)

Ready to Read: A Multisensory Approach to Language-Based Comprehension Instruction by
Mary Lupiani Farrell, Ph.D. and Francie M. Matthews, Ph.D. Copyright © 2010 by
Paul H. Brookes Publishing Co., Inc. All rights reserved.

Questions for Narrative and Expository Passages

Select a narrative story and expository text of 2–3 pages in length. Write 5 literal and 5 inferential questions related to each.

Literal Questions

Literal comprehension questions relate to information that is *explicitly* stated in the text. They are factual questions. The question words, *who, where, what,* and *when,* are often used in developing literal questions. These are examples of literal questions: Where or when did the story take place? Who is the main character of the story? What did John tell Lisa about his vacation? What happened after Tom went to bed?

Inferential Questions

Inferential questions require the reader to surmise something on the basis of something stated in the text, for example, draw a conclusion, infer a character's motivation or what he will likely do next, interpret his reason for saying something, determine why something happened, or infer something about a character's personality. To answer inferential questions, the reader has to interpret an unstated meaning from something in the text. Inferential questions often begin with the question words *why, how,* or *what do you think.* They often include qualifying terms such as *probably* and *likely* (What will probably happen?).

Ready to Read: A Multisensory Approach to Language-Based Comprehension Instruction by
Mary Lupiani Farrell, Ph.D. and Francie M. Matthews, Ph.D. Copyright © 2010 by
Paul H. Brookes Publishing Co., Inc. All rights reserved.

Glossary for Comprehension Needs Chart

LEARNER CHARACTERISTICS

Verbal reasoning   Learning with language.

Receptive vocabulary   The understanding of the meaning of single words presented auditorily.

Expressive vocabulary   The production of single words to express meaning.

Listening comprehension   The understanding of spoken connected language.

Fluency   The reading of connected text with fluency and expression.

Word attack   The reading of words primarily on the basis of sound–symbol association, including "nonsense" words.

Word identification   The reading of words largely on the basis of stored visual memory (sight vocabulary) as well as sound–symbol association.

Phonemic awareness   The discrimination of blending and segmenting speech sounds.

Visual spatial   Pertaining to perceiving, analyzing, synthesizing, recalling, and thinking with visual patterns.

Engagement   Reader's interest in and involvement with text.

Attention   Reader's ability to concentrate on task.

Working memory   Reader's ability to hold several facts or thoughts in memory while processing meaning.

Background knowledge   Reader's poor knowledge.

Note: Chart found on page 74.

READING COMPREHENSION

Reading comprehension   Overall understanding of written connected text.

Narrative text   Written connected text that is fiction, tells a story.

Expository text   Written connected text that provides factual information.

Literal comprehension   Understanding explicit information provided in text, such as the names of characters and sequence of events.

Inferential comprehension   The understanding of implicit information in text such as the main idea.

Before Reading

Before-reading strategies   Strategies that good readers use spontaneously before beginning to read text.

Access background knowledge   Activate prior knowledge to help understanding of new text. This will include "schema," or learned concepts, about the type of text (e.g., narrative vs. expository) as well as schema about the content of the text (e.g., mountains, baking).

Determine purpose for reading   Establish a focus for reading (e.g., study vs. leisure) in anticipation of what the reader is expected to glean from text; implementation of related strategies (e.g., adjusting reading rate, monitoring level of comprehension).

Preview text   Develop an overview of text (e.g., scan chapter headings or pictures) in advance to begin establishing a framework for constructing meaning of the text to be read.

Make predictions   Use a variety of cues, including background knowledge, to begin predicting, organizing, and constructing meaning from text.

Revise predictions as needed   Change predictions to conform to understanding gained from text.

During Reading/Narrative

Recognize key information   Identify setting, characters, problem.

Understand sequence   Comprehend temporal order of events.

Understand conflict   Understand the problems faced by the characters (e.g., finding a lost pet, obstacles to be overcome while making an important journey).

Retell   Retell story details in a manner reflecting accuracy and understanding.

Summarize   Identify and express the most important events in the story in an organized manner.

Understand emotions, beliefs   Identify and express understanding of character's motivation and feelings.

Understand genre   Identify and express understanding of type of story (e.g., fable, historical fiction).

Understand recurring themes   Identify and express understanding of underlying themes (e.g., bravery, loyalty, good vs. evil).

During Reading/Expository

Identify main idea   State the overall idea of the passage.

Locate details   Find the specific details that support the main idea.

Retell   Give a detailed oral or written recitation of text.

Summarize   Give an abbreviated recitation of text that paraphrases the main ideas.

Recognize and understand description   Identify and interpret description in text.

Recognize and understand sequence   Identify and understand sequence of events portrayed in text.

Recognize and understand classification   Recognize superordinate/subordinate relationships in text.

Recognize and understand compare ≠ contrast   Identify compare/contrast relationships in text as well as the connecting words that signal these relationships.

Recognize and understand cause and effect   Identify cause–effect relationships in text as well as the connecting words that signal these relationships.

After Reading/Elaborating Knowledge

Make connection to prior knowledge   Use relevant background knowledge to support comprehension of text.

Make inferences   Go beyond the literal meaning of the words or integrate clues to make educated guesses/assumptions about meaning.

Generate explanations that extend text information   Apply what is learned from text in a logical way; make a connection with text (text to self, text to world, text to other text).

Establish an opinion connected to text   Integrate facts learned in the text to form an opinion.

METACOGNITIVE SKILLS

Know strategies   Know reading strategies for different purposes.

Vary strategies according to purpose of reading and nature of text   Independently select/use appropriate strategy when reading.

Recognize comprehension breakdown   Recognize that one is confused about something just read or is not getting the full meaning.

Repair comprehension breakdown   Determine what should be done to repair the breakdown; select appropriate strategy.

VISUAL AIDS

Develop and use graphic organizers   Develop and use pictorial representations of text as a way to organize information acquired through reading.

Recognize common organizational patterns that support comprehension   Use bold words, headings, and captions to assist in the comprehension of text.

Index

Page numbers followed by *f* indicate figures; those followed by *t* indicate tables.